Stephen Crane in England
A Portrait of the Artist

Stephen Crane in England
A Portrait of the Artist

by

Eric Solomon

Ohio State University Press

To My Colleagues

Shephard Liverant   1927-1962

Alvin Scodel   1919-1964

Acknowledgments

THE RESEARCH FOR THIS VOLUME WAS aided by a grant from the American Philosophical Society. The staffs of the London Library, the British Museum, and the Columbia University Libraries were very helpful. I remain responsible for any flaws that exist in the book, but I am extremely grateful for the helpful readings of the manuscript given by my colleagues William Charvat, Roy Harvey Pearce, Julian Markels, Claude M. Simpson, and by Samuel Hynes. Miss Ida Mae Cornelius' typing was impeccable. My particular gratitude goes to Robert Estrich, best of chairmen, whose critical eye and supporting arm made this book possible.

Contents

Stephen Crane in England
A Portrait of the Artist

Introduction

"I spent ten years planning a study of Crane and ended by deciding there was no such animal, although I knew him for eleven years."—HENRY MCBRIDE *to* THOMAS BEER.[1]

"For one's self, all conveniently, there had been doors that opened—opened into light and warmth and cheer, into good and charming relations. . . ." HENRY JAMES.[2]

"He had friends there; he was understood and appreciated by the best minds in literature."— THOMAS RAYMOND.[3]

"He himself managed so conspicuously to elude the banquets and bouquets of his own calling that he left a very meagre tradition among 'literary people.' Had he . . . written a few papers about his works for reviews. . . ."—WILLA CATHER.[4]

H. G. WELLS GRIMLY BICYCLING through the night to get a doctor for the stricken Stephen Crane; Edward Garnett suggesting that Crane move to Surrey for a placid literary life; Ford Madox Ford engaging in a long literary conversation with Crane while in a rose garden; Henry James complacently eating a doughnut at a garden party arranged by Stephen Crane's "wife"; nine leading writers collaborating with Crane on a Christmas play to be presented in his home; and Joseph Conrad—

3

always Joseph Conrad—walking for hours through Hyde Park with Crane while describing Balzac's novels—such are the memorable images of Stephen Crane in England. The images are of an author among authors, a novelist who was the close companion of some of the most consciously artistic and dedicated craftsmen then writing fiction. But if these are the images brought forth by the years Stephen Crane spent in England (1897-1900, with the exception of nine months in Cuba while reporting the Spanish-American War), there were different views of the American Stephen Crane before he emigrated to England to live one-third of his writing career as an expatriate who was in close contact with serious and sensitive novelists.

"He knew peculiar people, he had a clinical curiosity about low life, he frequented barrooms, swore picturesquely, and played poker. He loaned money to prostitutes and consorted with outcasts."[5] Young Crane was a ballplayer who did not complete a year at the two colleges he attended, a penniless hanger-on

1 Ames W. Williams and Vincent Starrett, *Stephen Crane: A Bibliography* (Glendale, Calif., 1948), p. 7.

2 Henry James, "Introduction to *The Princess Casamassima*," *The Art of the Novel*, ed. R. P. Blackmur (New York, 1934), p. 61.

3 Thomas Raymond, *Stephen Crane* (Newark, N. J., 1923), p. 14.

4 Willa Cather, "Introduction," in *The Work of Stephen Crane*, ed. Wilson Follett (New York, 1926), IX, xiii.

5 Williams and Starrett, *Stephen Crane*, p. 10.

4

of a bohemian set of raffish commercial artists, a starving unknown. Even after the success of *The Red Badge of Courage* shot Crane into prominence, the pictures remain violent ones: Crane spurring his pony on through the desert to escape bloodthirsty Mexican bandits; Crane filibustering in Cuba and surviving a shipwreck; Crane having a liaison with the madam of a successful Florida bordello.

The two concepts—the wild young American soaking up experience and the thoughtful (still young) expatriate discussing life and art—seem contradictory. The contradictions accrue when we compare the literary intelligence displayed by the English writers of Crane's acquaintance to the casual ignorance flaunted by the Crane who could respond to a query about Mallarmé with the ironic comment that he didn't know much about Irish authors. If we accept the Crane "myth" and see him as a gloriously gifted, but undisciplined and somehow unconscious, instinctive artist[6] who blundered his way to literary success and popular fame, then the relationships with Ford and Wells, Conrad and James, must remain mysterious. It is only by attempting to realize the actual role of Crane that we can understand the true nature of these relationships—and, at the same time,

[6] In his autobiography, H. G. Wells attested to this view of Crane. "He had an intense receptiveness to vivid work; he had an inevitably right instinct for the word in his stories; but he had no critical chatter."—*Experiment in Autobiography* (London, 1934), p. 614.

5

begin to comprehend the basis of Crane's highly self-conscious literary art. By studying Stephen Crane's English *persona* we may discover a measure of truth about this complex character who resolved the contradictions of his public role as either adventurer or artist by his dedication to an adventurous art. Since there is insufficient literary comment on Crane's part to make his artistic personality self-evident,[7] we must draw inferences from the literary relations he developed after his arrival in England.

Stephen Crane's reasons for settling outside of the United States were largely negative. Unlike most expatriates, he did not write about the clash of American and European cultures. The contrasts that interested American authors from Washington Irving, James Fenimore Cooper, and Nathaniel Hawthorne, through Henry James, F. Scott Fitzgerald, and Ernest Hemingway were never treated in Crane's fiction. During the period of his voluntary exile, Crane continued to write of America—of the West, of rural New York State, of New York City. His pieces about England were journalism;[8] the American scene, along with his pictures of American soldiers at war in Cuba, provided the subjects for his major fiction. Unlike

[7] "Implicit in Crane's vision are ideas which Crane never began to make intellectually explicit."—Edwin Cady, *Stephen Crane* (New York, 1962), p. 69.

[8] In one of these pieces he showed a fine control of cockney dialect. See "At the Pit Door," *Philistine,* XI (September, 1900), 97-104.

6

Hawthorne's *The Marble Faun,* James's *The Portrait of a Lady,* or even Harold Frederic's *Mrs. Grundy,* Crane's novels and stories, except for *The O'Ruddy,* that were written while abroad did not have a foreign setting. For Stephen Crane, England was a refuge, not a subject.

It was not only the success of *The Red Badge of Courage* in England that attracted Crane to that country. His American success, though somewhat grudging, was assured by the time he left early in 1897 to cover the Greco-Turkish War. Starting from his beginnings in New Jersey, his early education at Claverack Academy, Lafayette College, and Syracuse University, during which time he concentrated more on his activities as an athlete and a newspaper stringer than as a scholar, the young Crane became a part of the New York artists' Bohemia while he searched for subject matter on the Bowery and wrote sketches about the lower depths of slum life in the city. While publishing his Sullivan County Sketches in the 1892 *Tribune,* the twenty-one-year-old Crane worked on *Maggie: A Girl of the Streets,* which he had printed privately the next year. Certainly these were years of struggle and privation, as they are for many young artists. When finally published, *Maggie* was badly received, although it did bring Crane to the attention of William Dean Howells and Hamlin Garland. Retaining the naturalistic technique in prose while starting a second

7

slum novel in 1894, Crane also wrote his unusual, short, bitterly ironic experiments in free verse which, when published in early 1895, brought him some notoriety, but, again, little appreciation. Indeed, these poems seemed to enrage newspapermen throughout the country. A spate of brutal parodies and burlesques sprang forth; *Town Topics* lumped together Crane and one Peregrine Popp: "Mr. Crane and Mr. Popp / Oh, for God's sake can't you stop / Won't you ever shut up shop?"[9]

The publication of Crane's masterpiece, *The Red Badge of Courage,* first in a short newspaper version, then as a book in October of 1895, literally changed his position overnight. Despite some cavils by disgruntled old soldiers who liked neither Crane's artistic effects nor the fact that his hero ran away, the novel brought the young writer fame. The novel was hailed for its realism, power, psychological impact, and brilliance of its prose after the English reviews were in, but the American criticisms were for the most part friendly and, of great importance for a starting novelist, widespread. Crane travelled west for the Bachellor syndicate, was lionized by Elbert Hubbard; by 1896, at the age of twenty-five, he had published six books—*Maggie, George's Mother, The Little Regiment* (Civil War stories), *The Third Violet* (a story of love among the artists), as well as the book of poems and the war novel. Periodicals

[9] *Town Topics* (New York), July 23, 1896.

8

were clamoring for his stories and articles and even willing to print his poems.

Fame brought notoriety. The newspapers seemed even less willing to accept the fact of Crane's successful novel than of his poems. Imitations of his poems continued, and a new genre, the "Stephen Crane Joke," appeared. One such was entitled "She May Be Right": "'I really believe that Stephen Crane is color blind,' said the girl who is given to cogitation. 'Why' asked the chorus. 'I just believe that all the red he sees is only greenness.'"[10] Another young naturalist, Frank Norris, parodied the war novel in "The Green Stone of Unrest." Laughter might have made Crane uncomfortable, but police persecution made his life unbearable. In a chivalric effort to protect a young lady from the police, he managed to attract the enmity of a corrupt New York detective force. It is not an exaggeration to say that the police drove him out of New York. Then, after reporting the Cuban insurrection, he fell in love with Cora Taylor, a woman he could certainly bring neither to New York City nor to his family in Port Jervis. Married to an Englishman who refused her a divorce, Cora was running a high-class brothel when Crane met her. She accompanied him to Greece in April, wrote some dispatches herself— which he "edited." Cora and Stephen were a permanent couple by the time he was ready to leave Greece.

[10] *Indianapolis Journal,* September 9, 1896.

Where to? For a number of reasons, England was the obvious haven. No newspapers nor police were against him there; quite the contrary. His work had made even more of a mark in England than in America. Publishers and writers alike were eager to meet him and help him get settled.[11] And the language barrier that made other parts of Europe seem out of the question for permanent residence was not an issue in England. Of most immediate importance, however, was the consideration that Cora would be accepted as Mrs. Stephen Crane, with no questions asked. Not only was there less prurient curiosity among the English journalists and authors whom Crane met than among their American counterparts, but the level of sophistication was such as to make acceptable Harold Frederic's odd domestic arrangement of two distinct households. Joseph Conrad had knocked about the world, Henry James was a bachelor, Ford Madox Ford and H. G. Wells were themselves separated or divorced. England also offered Crane a measure of intellectual freedom; there he escaped the inhibiting aura of morality that had seemed to stifle the reception of *Maggie* in the United States. "You can have an idea in England without

11 Heinemann's partner, Sidney Pawling, had written Crane on December 4, 1896, "We think so highly of your work—of its virility, actuality, and literary distinction that we have been pleased to take special pains to place it prominently before the British public." See Herbert F. West, *A Stephen Crane Collection* (Hanover, N. H., 1948), p. 19.

10

being sent to court for it."[12] According to Ford Madox Ford, London at that time was "a city of infinite curiosity as to new literary methods and of an infinite readiness to assimilate new ideas, whether they came from Paris by way of Ernest Dowson, from Poland by way of Conrad, or from New York or New England by way of Henry James, Stephen Crane. . . . "[13] It was in England, therefore, that Stephen Crane lived for the last three years of his short life, except for a nine-month reportorial jaunt to Cuba. He established homes in Surrey, first at Ravensbrook in Oxted and later, after his return from Cuba, in a rambling manor, Brede Place. Here Cora and he entertained his growing circle of friends, and here he wrote much of his best and, driven by debts, some of his worst work. And it was in England that he made the literary friendships that marked his growth as an artist.

Of course Stephen Crane knew many authors before he left the United States, but there was a significant difference between these and his later English friends. The American writers with whom Crane was on a friendly basis—Ripley Hitchcock, Richard Harding Davis, James Gibbons Huneker— were hardly serious novelists. To Hamlin Garland and William Dean Howells, Crane was an eager

[12] Thomas Beer, *Stephen Crane* (London, 1924), p. 217.
[13] Ford Madox Ford, "Techniques," *Southern Review,* I (July, 1935), 25.

protégé, a youthful initiate, grateful for advice and support. If Crane could see them for the time as his masters and could be at once worshipful and ostentatious, they, on their parts, while genuinely admiring Crane's talent, were necessarily avuncular and condescending. In England, barely two years later, Crane would be friendly with many gifted hacks like Robert Barr, A. E. W. Mason, H. B. Marriott-Watson, Edwin Pugh. He would communicate, however, with Conrad and James, not as a disciple to masters, but as an artist to artists, despite—perhaps because of—the obvious age differences.

There were many reasons for the close friendships between Stephen Crane and Conrad, James, Ford, and Wells. They all lived within a few miles of one another in southeastern England. Three of the five were expatriates, and all five were, in a way, out of the main currents of English social, ethical, and literary life. Crane's immediate success in England, which developed from the high sales and enthusiastic critical reception of *The Red Badge of Courage,* also served to make him an attractive and interesting figure. (The novel went through five English editions in three months, achieving a "noisy recognition.")[14] Crane's evident charm, his youth, his combination of bantam sureness and sensitive vulnerability, his later sickness that made him another

[14] Frederic Whyte, *William Heinemann* (London, 1928), p. 170.

"glorious boy" in the Keats-Chatterton tradition—all these elements would explain relationships similar to those he previously sustained with Howells and Garland. Yet unless we can wipe away the concept of Stephen Crane the brilliant improvisor, we cannot clarify the incongruities of the literary friendships of Crane. Despite the lack of any serious body of critical writing on Crane's part, we can piece together through a reconstruction of his sympathetic contacts with writers of the stature of Conrad and James, who wrote seriously and thoughtfully about the craft of the novel, an understanding of how Stephen Crane shared these writers' approaches to the art of fiction. Stephen Crane, then, for all his pose vis-à-vis Mallarmé, for all his scoffing at those who found French or Russian influences in his work, was not to be patronized by the writers who concentrated on delicate problems of form and structure. To Howells and Garland, dedicated realists, the sources of Crane's art would always be mysterious, as would the artist. To Ford, Wells, and Garnett, as well as to Conrad and James, Crane's work and Crane's person would be no more mysterious than their own. In Conrad's famous phrase, Stephen Crane was "one of us."

13

1

FROM THE MOMENT OF HIS ARRIVAL IN England, Stephen Crane was in touch with many of the most important writers of the day. Harold Frederic triumphantly escorted the best-selling author to lunch at the Savage Club and introduced him to James Barrie, Justin McCarthy, and Anthony Hope. Crane knew Henry Harland, the editor of the *Yellow Book* (who angered Crane by insisting that he must have read Stendhal), and was bored by conversation about Oscar Wilde whom Crane later described as "a mildewed chump. . . . Mr. Yeats is the only man I have met who talks of Wilde with any sense."[1] Although he was snubbed by George Meredith, Crane had tea with Algernon Swinburne who, according to Thomas Beer, entertained Crane with translations from a sixteenth-century manuscript. Maurice Hewlett called. W. E. Henley was charmed by Crane. And during his stay in England, Crane would not only form real friendships with American authors like Harold Frederic and Robert Barr, but

[1] Beer, *Stephen Crane*, p. 170.

15

also would become acquainted with English writers like E. V. Lucas, Edmund Gosse, R. B. Cunninghame Graham, W. H. Hudson, A. E. W. Mason, George Gissing.

Crane's success in England naturally pleased him and gave him confidence. "I have only one pride and that is that the English edition of *The Red Badge of Courage* has been recieved [sic] with great praise by the English reviewers. I am proud of this simply because the remoter people would seem more just and harder to win."[2]

While it is true that most of Crane's American reviews were very positive, the English reviews of *The Red Badge of Courage* were adulatory. The periodicals and newspapers hailed Crane's remarkable production for its extraordinary power that made previous descriptions of war seem like mere abstractions. The *Times* called him the Rudyard Kipling of the American army (this was a common comparison); the *Pall Mall Gazette* found Crane's insight and power of realization to amount to genius; and the *Daily Chronicle* felt that nothing in the whole range of literature was so searching in its analysis of the average mind under the stress of battle.[3]

[2] Crane to John N. Hilliard, January 2, 1896, R. W. Stallman and Lillian Gilkes (eds.), *Stephen Crane: Letters* (New York, 1960), p. 95.

[3] Excerpts from reviews printed on the endpapers of the second printing of Heinemann's first English edition of *The Red Badge of Courage.*

Strangely enough, the two periodicals that later printed Crane's best notices barely attended to *The Red Badge of Courage* when it first appeared. The *Athenaeum,* in an issue marked by a savage blast at Thomas Hardy's "titanically bad book," *Jude the Obscure,* simply noted Crane's novel among books received.[4] In a review by John Barrow Allen that praised fulsomely Robert Blatchford's *Tommy Atkins,* the *Academy* took Crane to task for his quaint, bantering style that became tiresome. "A serio-comic effect seems to be intended throughout . . . but the humour is scarcely of a sort to be appreciated by readers on this side [of the Atlantic]. . . . "[5] In its reviews of *The Little Regiment* and even *The Third Violet,* however, the *Athenaeum* used *The Red Badge of Courage* as a touchstone of Crane's genius, while the *Academy* went on through the years practically to adopt Crane. It was in its pages that Edward Garnett's appreciation first appeared; its editor, C. Lewis Hind, became one of Crane's friends and saw to it that each Crane publication was warmly praised by the journal's reviewers. In 1897, the *Academy* made up for its earlier lapse by attending to the rumor of Crane's death in Cuba with the comment that the new literature could ill afford to lose him. The article went on to call the production of *The Red Badge of Courage* "little short of marvelous.

[4] *Athenaeum* (November 23, 1895), 717.
[5] *Academy,* XLIX (February 15, 1896), 135.

Every page reads like the confessions of a veteran, every line reeks of battle smoke."[6]

Typical of the reception of the novel was the review in the *Guardian* that called *The Red Badge of Courage* "a new departure . . . throughout we feel that the analysis is true to life, and that this is what a battle really means to a private soldier. . . . Another blow has been given to the glamour and false charm of war."[7] The London *Bookman* praised Crane's genius for knowing how to apply the literal method of fiction. "The narrative is stamped with truth . . . quiet power."[8]

Crane did not, of course, receive only critical eulogies in England—despite the assertion of the New York *Bookman* (which had itself given an unfavorable notice to the novel) that the English critics "seem vying with one another in singing its praises until we understand that Mr. Crane bids fair to be the author of the hour in London."[9] The *Academy* in the 1897 *apologia* mentioned above contributed to the view of the unanimity of Crane's welcome. "Like so many American authors, he owes his success to British enthusiasm. It was not until *The Red Badge of Courage* was brought out in this country, in the autumn of 1895, that America 'found' its author. Mr.

[6] *Academy*, LI (January 16, 1897), 76.
[7] *Guardian*, No. 2617 (January 29, 1896), p. 178.
[8] *Bookman* (London), IX (January, 1896), 131.
[9] *Bookman* (New York), II (February, 1896), 469.

Crane would be the first to acknowledge his indebtedness to the English critics and the English public, who, with one accord, forced his name into well deserved prominence."[10] Not all the English reviewers showed wild enthusiasm over *The Red Badge of Courage,* however; the *Academy's* Allen was not the only dissenter. Just as Crane's later works met with a mixture of praise—for *The Open Boat* volume and the later novels—and grudging acceptance—for *Maggie* and *George's Mother* as well as the posthumously published *Whilomville Stories*—so *The Red Badge of Courage* had its English detractors.

An early review in the *National Observer* was, at best, lukewarm. The critic found Crane's style occasionally affected; the red sun pasted in the sky like a wafer was a particularly offensive image. The anonymity of the characters was confusing and meaningless. The reviewer concluded with the opinion that while not the best of Heinemann's "Pioneer Series," *The Red Badge of Courage* was a long way from the worst.[11] H. D. Traill's attack on the "new realism," a year later in the *Fortnightly Review,* singled out Stephen Crane as a special offender because of his half-truths. Although not as crude and tawdry as *Maggie,* the war novel was in no way realistic—because the author had never smelled powder.[12]

[10] *Academy,* LI (January 16, 1897), 76.
[11] *National Observer,* XV (January 11, 1896), 272.
[12] *Fortnightly Review,* CCCLXI (January 1, 1897), 63.

Certainly no negative American criticism went beyond the sustained attack on Crane included in Stephen Gwynne's article on "Novels of American Life" in the *Edinburgh Review* in 1898. Gwynne denied the reality of Crane's red haze and lurid dream of war; after all, Baden-Powell had said that man was more alert in combat. Therefore the psychological portrait of Henry Fleming was valueless. The style was clever but not agreeable: "words are heaped on words . . . till one feels as if one had been beaten about the head with epithets." Crane's basic flaw was a straining after effects; he was much less convincing than Kipling. Gwynne was even harsher on Crane's subsequent work, which he found either amazing in its futility (*The Third Violet*) or "a mass of revolting details." Gwynne held some hope that Crane might eventually mature, but at the time of writing all he offered was "a distorted psychology of combat and an exaggerated theory of style."[13]

Despite these chilly responses, the general tone of English reviews of Crane's work was warm. And in some cases the approval of *The Red Badge of Courage* was sufficiently ecstatic to make England seem to offer the young author a home where the public response to his work would be exhilarating. If the *Academy* and the *Athenaeum* were to remain Crane's supporters to the end of his career, the *Saturday Review* immediately discovered the war

---

[13] *Edinburgh Review*, CLXXXVII (April, 1898), 412-14.

book to be a masterpiece. In a note early in January, 1896, the *Saturday Review* anticipated its lengthy study of the novel with a brief paean: "We hope to treat this work at length next week; but we wish to draw our readers' attention to it at once, as containing, in our opinion, the most realistic description ever published of modern war . . . and this account is so impartial in its frankness that it comes to have the significance of universal truth."[14]

The next week's review, entitled "In the School of Battle," was a long, four-column study of the novel—strong in approbation. This book would tell England, in time of danger, of the innermost truths of battle. "The want finds the book as the opportunity finds the man." More intense than Tolstoy, more sustained than Kipling, more imaginative than Zola, more inspired than Merimée, Crane was the finest of all war novelists in depicting "how the sights and sounds, the terrible details of the drama of battle, affect the senses and the soul of man. Whether Mr. Crane has had personal experience of the scenes he depicts we cannot say from external evidence; but the extremely vivid touches of detail convince us that he has. Certainly if his book were altogether a work of the imagination, unbased on personal experience, his realism would be nothing short of a miracle." Crane's narrative skill, his poetic

[14] *Saturday Review*, LXXXI (January 4, 1896), 3.

diction, his realism, his "Sophoclean irony" made
The Red Badge of Courage a marvel.[15]

Even more exciting to Stephen Crane were the
glowing reports of his novel set forth by men who
became his acquaintances. The illustrator Joseph
Pennell steadily held that "the best story of the Battle
of the Wilderness, or any battle, is Stephen Crane's
Red Badge of Courage."[16] The novelist and journalist
Harold Frederic insisted in his dispatch to the *New
York Times* that Crane's work proved that inexperi-
enced creative artists wrote better novels than trained
correspondents. To Frederic, Crane's greatest accomplishment was the avoidance of clichés.[17] Another
popular novelist, H. B. Marriott-Watson, wrote a
glowing review of *The Red Badge of Courage* for the
Pall Mall Gazette. Calling his piece "The Heart of a
Soldier," he praised Crane's ability to synthesize the
carefully analyzed emotions of warfare. He granted
that Crane might seem too logical and cold-blooded,
but remarked on the "gift" that allowed Crane to
hold the interest of the reader without depending on
development of either plot or character to any great
extent. "His insight and his power of realization,"
concluded Marriott-Watson, "amount to genius."[18]

[15] *Saturday Review*, LXXXI (January 11, 1896), 44-45.

[16] Joseph Pennell, *The Adventures of an Illustrator* (Boston, 1925), p. 105.

[17] *New York Times Supplement* (January 26, 1896), p. 22.

[18] *Pall Mall Gazette*, XI (November 26, 1895), 4. Crane boasted that he could write circles around Marriott-Watson,

Remembering the brutal attacks made by American Civil War veterans like General A. C. McClurg[19] against *The Red Badge of Courage* because of its unreality, Crane must have been particularly pleased by the essay of George Wyndham, published in the *New Review* in January, 1896, and later reprinted as the introduction to Crane's *Pictures of War,* a volume of collected stories published by Heinemann. A noted scholar and political figure, Wyndham was a member of the Coldstream Guards, had fought

---

author of period novels of picaresque adventure of the type parodied in *The O'Ruddy.*

[19] McClurg was particularly angry with the English reviewers who, he felt, had praised Crane's novel only because of their anti-American bias. Sidney Brooks, an English journalist who was a freelance in 1896 and who eventually, in 1921, became editor of the *Saturday Review,* in an article entitled "Stephen Crane and the Critics" that appeared in the May 16 *Dial,* identified himself as one of the first English reviewers of *The Red Badge.* "Worse still—a quite damning fact, I fear—I even ventured to praise it." The English reviewer had thought the novel was a remarkable performance and in his review had tried to provide the evidence for this opinion, "But apparently it is a subtle insult for an Englishman to praise an American book. I used to think that a good book was a good book the whole world over" (*Dial,* XX [May 16, 1896], 297). Brooks proceeded to demolish McClurg's arguments: "But he saw the ambush we English reviewers were laying. Deep under our affected enthusiasm for this young writer was an intense desire to insult America" (298). McClurg's proofs of this plot were some senseless gibes against the Union Army that appeared three decades earlier in *Blackwood's.* The General's logic did not appeal to Brooks. Since thirty years ago "an ignorant British magazine talked of 'the swift-footed warriors of Bull's [*sic*] Run,'" and since Henry Fleming ran, the English reviewers praised *The Red Badge.* "To be sure! And so when I sat, pipe in mouth, a peaceable, jaded reviewer, happy to have come across a book

23

through the Suakim campaign, and was to become parliamentary under-secretary of state for war. This veteran soldier discovered Crane's picture of war to be accurate, his technique—particularly his use of point of view and his "brilliant and detached" imagery —admirable. "It leaves, in short, such indelible traces as are left by the actual experience of war." Like Zola, Crane "omits nothing and extenuates nothing."[20] While Crane must have been as pleased as was his friend Joseph Conrad[21] by Wyndham's response to the novel, the young author retained his aplomb. With his usual irony, he described Wyndham's conversation about the cowardice of American troops in combat (information that might well have been

---

above the dull dead level, my mind was really full of schemes for avenging Bunker Hill!" (298).

McClurg's misguided patriotism was equalled by his bad criticism. It was immaterial that the hero fought for the North, insisted Brooks who understood the universality of Crane's war novel. "If he had been an Englishman in the ditches before Sebastopol, or a Frenchman at Sedan, the book would have been just as remarkable, and the praise of the English journals no less warm" (298). Brooks also found the very passages that McClurg "crucified" to be among the finest bits of writing in the book.

[20] George Wyndham, "An Appreciation," Introduction to Stephen Crane, *Pictures of War* (London, 1898), p. xx. Wyndham wrote a friend the day after the novel appeared in England, "I want you to buy and read the 'Red Badge of Courage' by Stephen Crane. I have just reviewed it for the 'New Review' of January with enthusiasm."—*Letters*, ed. Guy Wyndham (Edinburgh, 1915), I, 337.

[21] Joseph Conrad, "His War Book," in *Last Essays* (London, n.d.), p. 342.

24

drawn from *The Red Badge of Courage*), "These matters were clearly proven to me last night at the Savage by a Mr. Wyndham who once met General Grant."[22]

England, then, gave the young author needed critical support. When his friends praised "The Bride Comes to Yellow Sky," Crane exulted, "I am so delighted when I am told by competent people that I have made an advance." His fellow writers realized "The Open Boat" was among Crane's best work, and he would contrast England to America: "Over here, happily, they don't treat you as if you were a dog, but give every one an honest measure of praise or blame. There are no disgusting personalities."[23] In England Crane found his confidence in his own powers supported by public acclaim. Karl Harriman, writing a few weeks before Crane's death, summed

[22] Beer, *Stephen Crane*, p. 183. The ever-zealous *Saturday Review* attacked Wyndham for his warlike writing: under "the spell of Mr. Crane's lurid and dominating style," Wyndham, according to the journal, tried to write like Crane, and failed (*Saturday Review*, LXXXVI [August 27, 1898], 280). Crane must have been even more pleased by a report in the *Illustrated London News* Literary Letter: "General Sir Evelyn Wood—than whom a braver man never lived—has expressed the opinion that Mr. Crane's work is quite the finest thing in that line that has ever been done, and that the intuitions of the boy who has never seen war are worth far more than the experiences of any writer known to him, even though he may have been in the thick of the fiercest battle."—Quoted in the *Critic*, 29 (July 25, 1896), 62.

[23] Letter to John Hilliard, prob. 1897, Stallman and Gilkes (eds.), *Letters*, p. 159.

25

up what England meant to Crane: "Stephen Crane lives in England for no reason in the world other than that he succeeds there. . . . They take the workmen within their ranks seriously in England. No literary man in Great Britain is regarded higher than this American, Stephen Crane. His friends, and such intimates as he cultivates, are among the best known of the writing guild."[24] He could meet his critics as equals, and he could even scoff at the pretensions to knowledge of one of his most favorable and influential supporters. Stephen Crane had come a long way in a short time, from being respectful to his critics, from the uncle-nephew relationships with Garland and Howells. In America, Crane was a bright young man, a writer to be watched. In England, he was an established author, a writer to be analyzed.

During his stay in England, Crane widened the amount of common ground on which he could meet his fellow authors by increasing his knowledge of English and Continental writers. Accustomed to scoffing at expectations that he must have read Zola and Tolstoy before writing *The Red Badge of Courage*, Crane found that even his casual acquaintances

[24] Karl Harriman, "A Romantic Idealist—Mr. Stephen Crane," *Literary Review*, IV (April, 1900), 86. See also "English Reviews of Stephen Crane," *Literary Digest*, XXI (July 7, 1900), 12: "The late Mr. Stephen Crane was . . . much more of a prophet in England than in his own country, and during his latter years he found it pleasant to make his home in a land where his work met such warm appreciation."

in England wouldn't believe the paucity of his knowledge of books. Nevertheless, by piecing together the scattered evidences of Crane's reading, we find that in addition to a rather full and careful knowledge of the writings of his intimates, Wells, Conrad, and James, Crane was reading fairly widely.[25]

The library at Brede had a good many contemporary authors: Kipling (whose style Crane said he had renounced), Stevenson (similar to Crane in many ways as a tubercular doomed to an early death and as a novelist who used violent action as a background to character study, and a man whose work Crane detested and parodied in *The O'Ruddy*), Henley (of whom Crane said that there was too much *I* in "Invictus"[26] and that his essay on Burns was "the best thing ever" that Henley wrote[27]), Yeats, Le Gallienne, Schreiner. There were also sets of standard

[25] According to Ford Madox Ford, "it was always difficult to feel certain what were Stevie's sources. I once heard him deny with tremendous emphasis that he had ever read a French book, and I once heard him deny with an almost equally tremendous emphasis that he had ever read a word of Henry James—but that was nothing but what you might call an antipathetic response to his surroundings. . . . He had read a number of French books in translation. . . . He certainly always commented with knowledge on any book of Flaubert's or any short story of de Maupassant's that I happened to mention. And I can say much the same about his acquaintance with the works of James."—"Stevie and Co.," in *New York Essays* (New York, 1927), p. 26.

[26] Beer, *Stephen Crane*, p. 239.

[27] Stephen Crane, "Concerning the English 'Academy,'" *Bookman* (New York), VII (March, 1898), 24.

27

classics—Shakespeare, Burns, Dryden, Gray, Long-fellow, Browning, Heine—that Crane might or might not have looked into.[28] According to Thomas Beer, in 1899, Crane was reading recent work—*Smoke, Peter Ibbetsen, Cashel Byron's Profession*—and told Henry James and Edmund Gosse what a magnificent book Anatole France's *The Procurator of Judaea* was.[29] In passing, Crane commented in conversation or in correspondence on Twain, Cooper, Poe, Harte, Cervantes, George Moore, and Hardy, and he wrote articles on Ouida and Harold Frederic that showed acute awareness of the authors' limitations. Perhaps Beer best describes the growth of Crane's literary interest and acumen while in England: "His reverence . . . was latterly on the drift away from men who could do things, and expending itself on men who knew things, on Huneker and on the Garnetts, whose progenitor 'bossed the British Museum and talked about old man Caxton as if they had been at school together.' "[30]

[28] Daniel G. Hoffman, *The Poetry of Stephen Crane* (New York, 1957), p. 32.

[29] Beer, *Stephen Crane*, pp. 224, 244.

[30] *Ibid.*, p. 223.

28

2

TO HIS CONTEMPORARIES IN ENGLAND, to the professional writers, editors, and publishers' readers who were Stephen Crane's companions, he seemed to be a great talent because of the work that he had done and would do—once he settled his social and business affairs. While Stephen and Cora Crane entertained first at Ravensbrook and then at Brede Place any writer who wanted a free meal, even the less perceptive observers like Edwin Pugh could understand that Crane held himself aloof from the "Indians" that surrounded him; he retained the artist's essential loneliness even in a crowd. Robert Barr, a competent journeyman who finally completed the posthumous *The O'Ruddy,* put on record the opinion that among all those writing in England in the late 1890's, Stephen Crane was the one most likely to produce the great American novel.[1] Similarly, Edward

[1] Robert Barr, quoted in *Bookman* (New York), XI (July, 1900), 405. A few days after Crane's death, Barr wrote, "I always fancied that Edgar Allan Poe revisited in the earth as

Garnett expected Crane to do "the" novel about the American journalistic world.[2] These men watched Crane's work with interest; E. V. Lucas, R. B. Cunninghame Graham, and others wrote to Conrad to praise "The Price of the Harness" as soon as Crane's story was published in *Blackwood's*.[3]

Harold Frederic, the novelist who had sent to the *New York Times* early in 1896 a glowing report of *The Red Badge of Courage*, became one of Crane's closest friends and remained so until Frederic died in 1898. The two families spent much time together, vacationing in Ireland, and passing evenings at each other's homes. It was Frederic who insisted that Crane write *Active Service*.[4] Frederic was extremely generous to Crane, not only introducing him to clubs and well-known writers, but also continuing to puff his literary genius. Frederic returned Crane's favorable notice of Frederic's work in the Chicago *Chap-Book*

S. Crane, trying again, succeeding again, failing again. . . ."— Barr to Karl Harriman, June 8, 1900, Stallman and Gilkes (eds.), *Letters*, pp. 286-87. For his part, Crane had a more limited opinion of Barr's talents: "a shrewd, capable, journalistic writer." —Thomas Beer, "Introduction," in *The Work of Stephen Crane*, VI, xii.

2 Garnett to Cora Crane, December 20, 1898, Stallman and Gilkes (eds.), *Letters*, p. 198.

3 Conrad to Crane, January 13, 1899, *ibid.*, p. 205. Ford Madox Ford asserted that Cunninghame Graham had the economy of resource "such as only Stephen Crane, himself aristocratically contemptuous, has otherwise attained."—"Techniques," p. 30.

4 Frederick Lewis Allen, *Paul Revere Reynolds* (New York, 1944), p. 51. Allen said that Crane "worshipped" Frederic.

by writing an adulatory review of *The Open Boat* for the *New York Times*. Calling the publication of the book the most important literary event of the week, Frederic reported that a nation of sailors appreciated Crane's great sea story. "The genius of this young son of America is being keenly felt here, and there is a quickening touch in this volume of stories which will put a new face on British appreciation. . . ." Frederic concluded his dispatch with a shrewd analysis of the reason for Crane's high position among English authors. "No living English prose writer of his years approaches his wonderful gift of original and penetrating observation, while no writer of English is today prouder of being an American. Possibly this steady, unswerving loyalty to his native land has helped to make him so many friends among Englishmen, who, even when men of letters, are sportsmen enough to like that man who stands up for his own regiment. Maybe Crane little knows himself what a powerful factor he has been of late in drawing England Westward."[5]

The extant descriptions of Stephen Crane in England set a sharp contrast to the portrayals of the exuberant young denizen of the Bowery slums, western barrooms, Florida bordellos. Nearly every writer who knew him commented on the seriousness of Crane's mien and his commitment to his craft. In the summer of 1899, C. Lewis Hind, the somewhat

[5] *New York Times* (May 1, 1898), p. 19.

31

precious editor of the *Academy,* saw Crane as "slender, quiet, and neat; unaffected, unromantic, and unobtrusive; always watchful yet always seeming weary and brooding, with the penetrating blue eyes of the visionary."[6] According to Hind, many English writers were proud to have in their midst the eminently successful Crane, this "young American who had captured literary England."[7] What struck Hind most acutely about Crane was the seeming incongruity of the young man withdrawn to the peace of Brede Place, yet "writing about wild deeds in outlandish places."[8] In other words, Hind realized that Crane was essentially an imaginative artist, the author of the brilliantly conceived *The Red Badge of Courage* rather than the later experiential *Wounds in the Rain.*

In Hind's opinion, Crane was primarily an observer. While his friends cavorted around Brede putting on a Christmas play, Crane, said Hind, sat in the corner, silent, watching. Hind was impressed by the attention to detail, by the search for the exact word that Crane showed in his anxiety to hit upon precisely the proper word to describe a bunch of bananas.[9] Hind's final compliment brought Crane

[6] C. Lewis Hind, *Authors and I* (London, 1921), p. 70.

[7] *Ibid.,* p. 71.

[8] *Ibid.,* p. 72.

[9] *Ibid.,* p. 72.

beyond the range of journalism: "His imagination worked better in a room than on a battlefield."[10]

It is easy to understand, however, why Crane had something of a public reputation as a hard-drinking, rambling bohemian. He did run up an incredible number of debts; he lavished liquor on his friends and hangers-on; he borrowed from Conrad, even from Conrad's publisher, to finance the jaunt to Cuba. And he did pose as a Bowery tough at times. The legend of Crane the crude roughneck was perpetuated by men like Edwin Pugh, a popular novelist who was clearly one of the parasites on Brede Place.[11] In a remarkably ill-tempered article twenty-five years after Crane's death, Pugh characterized Crane as another Poe—stressing the decadent connotations.[12]

[10] *Ibid.*, p. 74.

[11] In the Brede Place Visitors Book, now in the Crane Collection of the Butler Library at Columbia University, Pugh wrote on November 25, 1899, "If it is true that by increasing other folks happiness we increase our own, what a store of joy must there be in this old house in which I have lived and worked for the shortest week of my life."

[12] Pugh attempted to demolish the story of Joseph Conrad's friendship with Crane. According to Pugh's version, Conrad patronized the younger writer, and Crane, for his part, was ironic toward Conrad's affected "humility." Pugh's argument appeared to be a special one: "And lest these conclusions should seem a little invidious I would add that though unquestionably Conrad was the first friend Crane made in England . . . he was much more frank and generally in sympathy with me than he seems to have been with any of his other friends."— "Stephen Crane," *Bookman* (New York), LXVII (December, 1924), 163. Pugh took offense because Conrad comprehended the side of Crane that Pugh couldn't reach.

Thus, Crane was "beautiful and brave and careless"; he played handball like a machine-gun, said Pugh; he wandered around Brede humming, "'I'll be there, I'll be there! When the Hully Gee is calling I'll be there—Sure as you're born!'"[13] Pugh's version of Crane's conversation was colorful but missed Crane's ironies. Pugh showed little understanding of the scope of Crane's gay humor that served as a release from the grim vision of life about which he privately pondered and wrote. "'Say, when I planted these hoofs of mine on Greek soil, I felt like the hull of Greek literature, like one gone over to the goldarned majority. I'd a great idea of Greece. One catches these fleas at Syracuse, N'York. So I said to the chocolate-box general of the Greek army: "Can I go into the fighting line?" And he says to me like a Denver Method: "Not in those trousers, sonny."' . . . Then Stevie paused, filled, drained his glass. . . . "[14] Here, then, was the Crane of legend, who appeared to fit the stereotype of casual spinner of anecdotes. Pugh partially realized that this pose on Crane's part was put on and off. As Ford Madox Ford assumed that Crane played the Western cowpuncher role mainly to shock and embarrass Henry James,[15] so Edwin Pugh understood that Crane affected a

13 Pugh, "Stephen Crane," p. 163.

14 *Ibid.*, p. 163.

15 Ford Madox Ford, *Return to Yesterday* (London, 1924), p. 29.

34

Yankee accent when telling a story. Underlying all Pugh's reports of Crane the humorist was the sense of his loneliness, "self-reliant, self-contained, immutably self-sufficient."[16]

While Crane could appear as simply a boon companion to many of his friends, his relationship to the quiet, scholarly Edward Garnett was more complex. In all probability, Crane took up his first residence in England in a villa called Ravensbrook at Oxted, Surrey, in order to be near Garnett,[17] who was only three years older than Crane. At any rate, Conrad, Galsworthy, and Crane often met at the Garnett home, The Cearne.[18]

Edward Garnett, who as critic and essayist gave spiritual and practical aid to Conrad, Galsworthy, T. E. Lawrence, and many other young writers with whom he came in contact through his position as publisher's reader for the houses of Fisher, Unwin, Heinemann, and Jonathan Cape, was basically a sensitive, careful man of letters, "an articulate literary conscience . . . with . . . almost uncanny insight."[19] He was interested in realism, in technique, in what he called veracity; and, above all, he insisted upon development and growth in his young writers.[20] He

16 Pugh, "Stephen Crane," p. 163.

17 David Garnett, *The Golden Echo* (London, 1954), p. 62.

18 H. E. Bates, *Edward Garnett* (London, 1950), p. 21.

19 Joseph Conrad, "Stephen Crane," *Last Essays*, p. 332.

20 Carolyn G. Heilbrun, *The Garnett Family* (New York, 1961), pp. 99, 100.

recognized at once what he considered to be Stephen Crane's chief weaknesses: "He wrote too much, he wrote against time, and he wrote while dunned for money."[21] Garnett also disapproved of the offensive crew of journalists with whom Crane surrounded himself.

Garnett certainly helped to continue the tradition of Crane as a slapdash, intuitive—even lucky—master of language. When reprinting in 1922 his *Academy* appreciation of Crane (which Conrad called "precisely just . . . showing all there is,"[22] and "with a well-balanced sympathy with the blind, pathetic striving of the artist towards a complete realization of his individual gift"[23]), Garnett insisted that Crane never had any sense of self-criticism. He never knew what his best work was[24] (an emotional failing attributable to many artists); "Crane's genius, his feeling for style were wholly intuitive, and no study had fostered them."[25] The charm, the impressionistic light touch

[21] Edward Garnett, "Stephen Crane," in *Friday Nights* (London, 1922), reprinted and expanded from *Academy,* LV (December 17, 1898), p. 204.

[22] Conrad to Garnett, December 18, 1898, *Letters from Joseph Conrad 1895-1924,* ed. Edward Garnett (Indianapolis, 1928), p. 148.

[23] Conrad, "Stephen Crane," p. 332.

[24] H. E. Bates said that Crane never knew that "The Open Boat" was his finest story (H. E. Bates, "Stephen Crane: A Neglected Genius," *Bookman* [London], LXXXI [October, 1931], 10).

[25] Garnett, "Stephen Crane," p. 204.

of *The Third Violet,* the brief sketching of the surface of life in *George's Mother,* were all of a piece with Crane's extravagant way of life and overindulgence in journalism.

Nevertheless, despite the fact that Crane's casual approach to the world and some of his superficial work disturbed Garnett greatly, his basic assessment of Crane—the man and the work—revealed a split in Garnett's approach. He and Conrad may have agreed that there was a peculiarly limited range to Crane's work; they also agreed that his genius was unique— and not careless.[26] Garnett stressed Crane's desire for accuracy, his *controlled* irony, his combination of power and delicacy, all qualities to be attained only by a careful craftsman, one whose work could be mentioned in the same breath with that of Dostoevsky.[27]

Crane was enough of an historian to collect interviews with Civil War veterans, according to Garnett, and to be able to recall totally the matter-of-fact responses he had received. And his use of irony was delicate, "deriding the swelling emotions of the self. It is his irony that checks the emotional intensity of his delineation, and suddenly reveals passion at high tension in the clutch of the implacable tides of life. It is the perfect fusion of these two forces of passion and irony that creates Crane's spiritual background,

[26] *Ibid.,* p. 202.
[27] *Ibid.,* p. 217.

37

and raises his work, at its finest, into the higher zone of man's tragic conflict with the universe."[28]

Long after Crane's death, Edward Garnett would continue to support his friend's work and to blame American critics for their "grudging, inadequate recognition of the most original genius it has produced in story-telling."[29] Garnett never grew tired of praising Crane's virtues, and the essence of his argument was that Crane was a brilliantly controlled master of careful effects. Conventional critics in 1916, accustomed to melodramas and historical romances or solidly factual novels, appreciated Crane's achievement no more than they understood what Conrad, James, or Ford were attempting to do within the boundaries of fiction. Garnett realized that no matter how active and powerful Crane's writing was, it could be also as cool, detached, and formal as that of James. Even an early piece of reportage like "An Experiment in Misery" seemed to Garnett to represent the kind of pure art that "infects one with all the artistic joyousness that is traditionally associated with Botticelli's Spring."[30] Garnett wrote Alfred Knopf in 1921, "I think of writing 'A Letter to an American Editor' on the subject of America's neglect of Crane

[28] *Ibid.*, pp. 213-14.

[29] Edward Garnett, "Some Remarks on English and American Fiction," *Atlantic Monthly*, XIV (December, 1914), 748.

[30] Edward Garnett, "A Gossip on Criticism," *Atlantic Monthly*, CXVII (February, 1916), 179.

and other writers."[31] And before Joseph Conrad wrote his powerful introduction to Thomas Beer's life of Crane, Conrad was advised by Garnett to devote part of the essay to Crane's style: " . . . it's perfection at its finest."[32] Garnett sent T. E. Lawrence a copy of *Maggie,* and Lawrence gleefully reported back to his mentor that he had found a copy of *The Red Badge of Courage.*[33] Garnett was delighted that the young H. E. Bates had somehow picked up knowledge of Crane's work.[34] This permanent commitment to Crane's memory testified not only to Edward Garnett's affection for his friend Stephen Crane but also to an admiration of his artistry, which, as Garnett wrote in his *Academy* obituary of Crane, was supreme and very modern.[35]

[31] Heilbrun, *The Garnett Family,* p. 102.

[32] *Ibid.,* p. 130.

[33] Lawrence to Garnett, September 25, 1933, *The Letters of T. E. Lawrence,* ed. David Garnett (New York, 1939), p. 777.

[34] Bates, *Edward Garnett,* p. 15. Bates later took up Garnett's role as defender of Crane's reputation and wrote that Crane was "unromantic, bitter, imaginative, perfect in detail and, more important still, perfect in atmosphere." Bates went on to praise "his instinct for arresting impressions, his genius for colloquial conversation, his unerring knowledge of human passions. . . . His compressed style had a compelling intensity . . . economy of material, a perspective and a sense of irony and justice." Like Crane's early English reviewer who called his irony Sophoclean, Bates averred that Crane reached the profound finality of Greek tragedy (Bates, "Stephen Crane," pp. 10-11).

[35] *Academy,* LIX (August 11, 1900), 116.

3

OF ALL ENGLISH WRITERS WHO WERE Stephen Crane's friends and advocates, H. G. Wells left perhaps the clearest report of the fascination inspired by the American novelist. What interested Wells from the start was the mixture of violence and repose, the tension between active service and peaceful contemplation that marked Crane's work as well as his personality. Admiring Crane first of all because he broke away from the genteel literary tradition of the Victorians, Wells recalled Crane as "a lean, blond, slow-speaking, perceptive, fragile, tuberculous being, too adventurous to be temperate with anything and impractible to an extreme degree. He liked to sit and talk, sagely and deeply. How he managed ever to get to the seats of war to which he was sent I cannot imagine."[1]

Wells's description of Crane as author helps to clarify the connection between Crane and Henry James. Wells was angry that public pressures forced

[1] Wells, *Experiment*, p. 612.

Crane to become a war correspondent. Not realizing that it was necessary for Crane's self-respect and his fascination with death to test himself in combat, nor, indeed, that Crane was a fairly good reporter, H. G. Wells delineated Crane's approach to writing in terms that could easily be applied to James, terms that were far removed from the familiar version of Crane the casual performer setting down memories of violent action. Wells stressed how Crane "could sit at home and, with nothing but his wonderful brain and his wonderful induction from recorded things," create. And Wells went on to aver, just as Garnett would, that Crane was "a fastidious and careful worker."[2] Like all of Crane's contemporaries, Wells firmly believed that the best work was yet to come. The buoyant and burly Englishman couldn't believe that Crane would not conquer tuberculosis as easily as Wells himself had: " . . . what business have you in the Valley? It isn't midday yet and Your Day's Work handsomely started I admit, is still only practically started."[3]

[2] H. G. Wells, "Stephen Crane from an English Standpoint," *North American Review*, CLXXI (August, 1900), 236, 237. At this point in his career, Wells upheld a concept of serious fiction, and, as Gordon Ray has shown, called for standards that would enable the critic to attend to structure and design. See Gordon N. Ray, "H. G. Wells Tries To Be a Novelist," in *Edwardians and Late Victorians* (New York, 1960), p. 111.

[3] Wells to Crane, April 22, 1900, Stallman and Gilkes (eds.), *Letters*, p. 276.

Wells was always proud that "however obscurely, I also was in the first chorus of welcome that met his coming."[4] When the *Academy* collected, for its 1896 Christmas book number, votes from noted English authors for the best books of the year, Wells included two novels by Stephen Crane on his list, *Maggie* and *George's Mother*.[5] In the *Saturday Review* four months earlier—the journal that had given *The Red Badge of Courage* a rapturous welcome—Wells published a warm review of *George's Mother*. He was excited by the promise of novelty in Crane's work, by his use of inner monologue; Wells understood the strength and compassion implicit in the tightly written tale: " . . . it is bare story and nothing beyond. There are no purple passages, no decorations, no digressions."[6] Even before he met Crane, Wells was convinced that contrary to Garnett's view that Crane was incapable of self-criticism, the American author must be a self-conscious craftsman. "Mr. Crane, albeit much more of a theoretical product than critics here have recognized, is evidently a young man of very exceptional ability."[7]

For the November 28 issue of the *Saturday Review*, Frank Harris wrote an uncomplimentary review of *Maggie* while the book was out on assignment to

[4] Wells, "Stephen Crane," p. 234.

[5] *Academy*, LI (January 16, 1897), 76.

[6] H. G. Wells, "The New American Novelists," *Saturday Review*, LXXXII (September 5, 1896), 263.

[7] *Ibid.*, p. 263.

43

Wells. In this issue no review of *Maggie* appeared; Arthur Morrison's *A Child of the Jago* was favorably noticed as a slum novel; and two weeks later, Wells insisted on publishing his own review of *Maggie*.[8] Hardly overwhelmed himself by the novel, Wells wrote a rather imperceptive study of *Maggie* that found Crane's novel to be of lighter weight than Morrison's.[9] Wells was inclined to take Crane to task for his alertness and cleverness and seemed to prefer the quiet power of Morrison to the self-awareness of the American author.[10] While Wells praised the emotional impact of the powerful final chapter of *Maggie*, he was put off by the color of Crane's impressionism; the barroom brawl excessively suggested the palette dipped in vodka. If Wells's review was complimentary in comparison to that of Frank Harris, the latter's must have been savage indeed.

When he considered *The Red Badge of Courage* and *Maggie* together, Wells fell into a certain confusion, praising *Maggie* for the wrong reasons and attacking the war novel on equally incorrect grounds. Doubting the source of Crane's apparent strength, Wells wondered whether *The Red Badge of Courage*

[8] Gordon N. Ray, "H. G. Wells's Contributions to the *Saturday Review," Library*, XVI (March, 1961), 32.

[9] H. G. Wells, "Another View of *Maggie," Saturday Review*, LXXXII (December 19, 1896), 655.

[10] Morrison's style and content seem indeed heavier—awkward and melodramatic also. Morrison completely lacked Crane's ironic touch that saved *Maggie* from sentimentality or rage.

displayed merely stress. "Strength and gaudy colour rarely go together; tragic and sombre are well nigh inseparable. One gets an impression from the 'Red Badge' that at the end Mr. Crane could scarcely have had a gasp left in him—that he must have been mentally hoarse for weeks after it. But here he works chiefly for pretty effects, for gleams of sunlight on the stagnant puddles he paints. He gets them, a little consciously perhaps, but . . . far more effectively than he gets anger and fear. And he has done his work, one feels, to please himself." This last statement seems critically vague, unless pleasing himself means developing his own art and resources. Wells's conclusion was equally fuzzy: "His book is a work of art, even if it is not a very great or successful work of art. . . . "[11]

Wells was particularly interested in the growth of Crane's art. For his part, Wells slowly moved from considering himself a novelist and from paying considerable attention to matters of form and structure, to the position of a polemicist who used the novel largely as a means of communicating ideas. Crane was always primarily a formal technician in Wells's view, and he was able to appreciate the developing artistry of Crane's technique. For example, in 1898, Wells announced that Crane's war story "Death and the Child" "comes as near perfection as one could wish . . . as subtle and convincing an invention as we

[11] Wells, "Another View of *Maggie*," p. 655.

45

can recall; and the story, handled with admirable simplicity and skill, is the most artistic thing Mr. Crane has yet accomplished."[12] Two years later, Wells criticized Crane for putting too much *in* the story, for making a concession to the type of literary criticism that demanded explicitness and generalization (as Wells usually did) and did not understand restraint and ambiguity (as Wells in his arguments with James usually did not).[13]

Thus, when Wells turned to consider Crane's collection of short stories *The Open Boat* in 1898, he was most attracted by Crane's increasing technical mastery. Wells thought that "not the least value of the present volume consists in the fact that it shows with unmistakable plainness how earnestly he is endeavouring to find his style, to arrive at the true formula of self-expression."[14] The statement is of real importance, coming as it did from a man who knew Crane well. This contemporary testimony strengthens the concept that Crane, while in England, was diligently working through problems of the art of fiction —just as, elsewhere in the rolling Surrey hills, James,

[12] *Saturday Review,* LXXXV (June 11, 1898), 785. Although Mr. Ray does not include this article among Wells's contributions to the *Saturday Review,* the internal evidence of Wells's style and the similarity in tone and content to many of the judgments he made two years later in his *North American Review* piece convince me that this review was Wells's work.

[13] Wells, "Stephen Crane," p. 235.

[14] *Saturday Review,* LXXXV (June 11, 1898), 785.

Ford, and Conrad were seeking new approaches to fictional representation.

In this same review, Wells shifted ground on *The Red Badge of Courage,* praising it much more generously than he had previously done. Crane had a new voice, a voice that had something to say. "The story told was engrossing, compelling; it revealed a section of the psychology of war which Mr. Kipling had not shown us." Again Wells insisted upon Crane's increasing interest in form and function: " . . . it proclaimed itself the work of a man who, already master of his material, lacked only mastery of his style."[15]

The stories showed this mastery of style. For Wells, it was Crane the creator of imagined situation who counted more than Crane the recorder of experienced event. Thus "The Bride Comes to Yellow Sky" seemed more impressive than "The Open Boat." The article closed with the same judgment of Crane that Wells would apply to Henry James during their lengthy argument about the purposes of fiction. Wells urged the young American author, just as he would urge his older compatriot, to deal with "more passionate issues."[16] When Wells accused Stephen Crane of lacking critical chatter and of being unable to talk sensibly about his contemporaries,[17] the politically,

15 *Ibid.,* p. 785.
16 *Ibid.,* p. 785.
17 Wells, *Experiment,* p. 614.

47

scientifically, and historically conscious Wells was again lumping Crane with Conrad and James. To Wells, critical chatter meant politics and philosophy—hardly Crane's forte—not "style," "luminous impressions." That Crane never discussed serious ideas with Wells was hardly to be wondered at. Wells found most of his novelist friends "impulsive, unco-ordinated, wilful. Conrad, you see, I count uneducated, [as I do] Stephen Crane, Henry James. . . . "[18] As he had done earlier with Crane, Wells found James, Conrad, and Ford all working outside the English tradition of the novel despite their "trained skill and anxious intensity."[19]

Wells's major hymn of praise for Crane and his work, the important essay "Stephen Crane from an English Standpoint," appeared in the *North American Review* shortly after Crane's death. In addition to the distinctively American qualities of freedom, directness, and freshness, Wells praised Crane's stylistic excellence and described it in terms that would have been equally applicable to the type of fiction cultivated by Conrad and James. Here Wells was completely willing to grant the fundamental importance of technique—particularly impressionistic and delicate selectivity. Crane could achieve warmth and tenderness in his slum stories without becoming emotional; he could reach luminous perfection ("The

[18] *Ibid.*, p. 620.
[19] *Ibid.*, p. 660.

48

Wise Men"); and his "brilliant fragments" were better than any longer efforts conventional critics might want to substitute for Crane's sketches and anecdotes.[20]

"The Open Boat," said Wells, was the cream of all Crane's work. Again it was the *restraint* that impressed Wells more than the power, the discipline and control more than the color and imagery.[21] Even *The Third Violet* met with Wells's approval since, despite the superficiality, it was forceful, objective, and in a manner "curiously hard and unsympathetic."[22]

As in *The Red Badge of Courage* where Crane omitted mention of the causes and justifications of the war (as Wells himself did in his *The War of the Worlds*[23]), in *The Third Violet* Crane avoided de-

[20] Wells, "Stephen Crane," p. 239.

[21] *Ibid.*, p. 237.

[22] *Ibid.*, p. 240.

[23] Wells's 1898 novel *The War of the Worlds* might have owed something to Stephen Crane; the scenes of panic remind one of "Death and the Child." But see Bernard Bergonzi, *The Early H. G. Wells* (Manchester, England, 1961), p. 130: Wells's scenes of war "are all the more remarkable for being written out of pure imagination: they remind one of the similar gift displayed by Wells's friend, Stephen Crane, in the writing of *The Red Badge of Courage*." There seem to be passages in Wells's later novel *Mr. Britling Sees It Through* that recall Crane more strongly: " . . . search-lights flashed luridly, and men darkly seen in silhouette against red flames ran with fixed bayonets and slipped and floundered over the mud, and at last, shouting thinly through the wind, leaped down into the enemy trenches."—*Mr. Britling Sees It Through* (London, 1926), p. 360.

49

scriptions of love. "Any richness of allusion, any melody or balance of phrase, the half quotation that refracts and softens and enriches the statement, the momentary digression . . . are not merely absent, but obviously and sedulously avoided."[24] From this passage, one could conclude that Wells found Crane to be much more selective than Conrad who was inclined to lush descriptions or James who usually over-complicated his prose with qualifications.

Indeed, in concluding his direct argument with the Master on the subject of the Jamesian school of fiction, Wells, after vigorously and destructively belaboring James, Conrad, and Ford, echoed Edward Garnett's belief that Crane's reputation was shamefully underrated. " 'America,' said Boon, 'can produce such a supreme writer as Stephen Crane—the best writer of English for the last half-century. . . . But America won't own such children. . . . She'll sit never knowing she's had a Stephen Crane.' "[25]

[24] Wells, "Stephen Crane," p. 242. Ford Madox Ford was inclined to agree with Wells's evaluation of *The Third Violet*: " . . . his one ewe lamb amongst his books . . . I have been preaching the claims of that book for years."—"Techniques," p. 26.

[25] H. G. Wells, *Boon* (London, 1915), p. 144.

4

IT WAS NOT FORD MADOX FORD'S FAULT that Stephen Crane was underrated. Throughout the 1920's and 1930's, Ford continued vigorously to praise Crane the man and Crane the writer. In articles, literary reminiscences, histories of literature, and autobiographies, Ford wrote of "Stevie" in a tone of admiration that verged on adulation. Even more Crane's contemporary than were most of his other English companions (Ford was four years younger than Crane), Ford did not let the passage of time dim his personal affection nor his critical appreciation for his dead friend. To Ford, Stephen Crane was the archetype of the dedicated artist, the brilliant manipulator of words, and the isolated romantic. Above all, Crane was a stylist.

An immediate problem, of course, is posed by the use of Ford Madox Ford as an authority. To put it bluntly, Ford's statements were often exaggerated, embroidered—or, indeed, invented. Edward Garnett, for example, testified that Ford's book on Conrad was filled with inaccuracies, most of which redounded to Ford's greater glory.[1] Richard Aldington recalled that "Ford entertained us with amusing but not necessarily literally accurate stories of . . . Conrad, Henry James. . . ."[2] And John Peale Bishop realized that Ford's anecdotes were "admirable fiction."[3] It is obvious that Ford not only often contradicted himself in his repeated versions of a single incident, but also that he was often simply wrong. It was possible that Ford heard from Crane that he read Zola's *La Débâcle* in French along with most of De Maupassant and Flaubert's *Education sentimentale*,[4] for Crane was certainly equal to such an obvious sarcasm. Ford, however, certainly knew better than to present this statement as evidence that Crane's other denials of a reading knowledge of French were mere modesty. Although Crane did meet many well-known authors, only Ford included George Bernard Shaw and Professor Hobson among the highbrow Fabians who received Crane. Not satisfied that Crane had dined at the Savage Club, Ford added the Savile and the

[1] Edward Garnett, "Review of Ford Madox Ford, *Joseph Conrad*," *Nation and Athenaeum*, XXXVI (December 6, 1924), 366.

[2] "Homage to Ford Madox Ford," *New Directions 7* (Norfolk, Conn., 1942), p. 457.

[3] *Ibid.*, p. 462.

[4] Ford Madox Ford, *The March of Literature* (New York, 1938), p. 829.

Devonshire to the list.[5] Surely these assertions rank with what Edward Dahlberg has called Ford's "ample, preposterous, and bellied remarks about literature."[6]

If Ford was not always faithful to fact, however, most of his intimates contended that there were germs of truth in his reports, that while the facts might be astray, the impressions would probably be accurate. His biographer presented a fair statement of Ford's veracity: "Ford regarded facts as raw material, to be handled by the artist with complete freedom for the purpose of enhancing whatever effect it was his desire to create. Thus he never troubled to verify names or dates and frequently blended invention with his verbal or visual memories. At the same time, where his artistic conscience was concerned, as in impressions of character, his perception was keen and his integrity above suspicion."[7] Herbert Gorman was assured that Ford's stories were always half accurate despite his fabrications, and if not true, they should have been— since his exaggerations often contained a deeper truth.[8] Perhaps Christopher Morley set forth the best apology for Ford's method. Speaking of the

[5] Ford Madox Ford, *Mightier Than the Sword* (London, 1938), p. 46.

[6] "Homage," p. 467.

[7] Douglas Goldring, *The Last Pre-Raphaelite* (London, 1948), p. 29.

[8] Herbert Gorman, "Ford Madox Ford: The Personal Side," *Princeton University Library Chronicle*, IX (April, 1948), 121.

53

Conrad biography, Morley stated that the suggestions were more important than the details. If Conrad didn't throw teacups into the fire, he probably looked as if he wanted to so strongly that "Ford conveyed it to us by what was probably an actual misstatement and a shining intellectual veracity."[9] Thus some of Ford's pronouncements about Stephen Crane and Henry James need not be taken literally. Crane probably did not continually ride around Surrey on a huge coach-horse, often stopping at James's door to shock his guests by crude Bowery slang; Ford's veracity was even more questionable when he described Crane's raffish friends inundating Lamb House, poking James in the ribs, and borrowing money from him. Still, there were aspects of reality in Ford's accounts. Crane sometimes did like to tease James; James was, as Crane's real friends were, in all probability disturbed by the heap of parasites on Brede Place. If the facts were wrong, the impressions were not. As Ford himself once said, "Nothing could be more literally false but nothing could be more impressionistically true."[10] When Ford said that James called Crane " 'My young compatriot of genius,' "[11] the words might be incorrect, but the sense of James's feeling for Crane, as revealed in James's letters, was absolutely true. Ford's impressions of the American

[9] "Homage," p. 476.

[10] Ford, "Techniques," p. 24.

[11] Ford, *Return to Yesterday*, p. 29.

54

writer, his knowledge of Crane's artistic temperament, his assessment of the literary achievement, and his estimate of the relations between Crane, Conrad, and James are all valuable and incisive.

Ford's memories of his friendship with Crane were naturally tinted by a nostalgic glow of emotion for his dead comrade whom he considered a marvelous novelist and a pure spirit. The young English writer and his American counterpart had much more in common with each other than with Wells, Conrad, or James. They were both precociously prolific, both established authors by the age of twenty-five. They wrote free verse as a release from prose, without paying much attention to poetic form. And both Ford and Crane left four or five great works among a mass of ephemeral chaff and potboilers. As Ford put it, " . . . our ideas about life and letters were pretty similar."[12]

Ford Madox Ford claimed that Edward Garnett introduced Crane to Ford so that two promising new authors could become acquainted.[13] He soon formed a comfortable friendship with Crane.[14] Ford frequently bicycled over to Rye to call on James or

[12] Ford, *Mightier Than the Sword,* p. 44.

[13] Ford Madox Ford, *Joseph Conrad* (London, 1924), p. 16.

[14] In one of his memoirs, Ford provided a map of Sussex with Crane in the center, surrounded by Wells, Hudson, James, Hardy, Galsworthy, Conrad, and Kipling (Ford, *Joseph Conrad,* p. 20).

the "cranky" Stephen Crane.[15] Crane rarely commented on the personalities of any of his literary acquaintances, but he accepted Ford, ego and all. In a letter to Sanford Bennett, Crane asserted, "You must not be offended by Mr. Hueffer's manner. He patronizes Mr. James. He patronizes Mr. Conrad. Of course he patronizes me and he will patronize Almighty God when they meet, but God will get used to it, for Hueffer is all right."[16]

If Crane considered Ford to be "all right," Ford more than reciprocated the feeling. He found Crane "the most beautiful spirit" he had ever known. For all his crochets and impostures, Crane was "honourable, physically brave, infinitely hopeful, generous, charitable to excess, observant beyond belief, morally courageous, of unswerving loyalty, a beautiful poet— and of untiring industry."[17] Frail, idealistic, freedom-loving, and truthful, Crane reminded Ford of Shelley.

[15] Violet Hunt, *The Flurried Years* (London, 1926), p. 41.

[16] Ford Madox Ford, *Portraits from Life* (Boston, 1937), p. 45. Ford continued to patronize Mr. James by stating that James envied "poor Stevie" for his gifts of popularity (Ford, "Techniques," p. 26). Ford's thoughts about this letter are of interest. "I suppose this air of patronage in my manner came from the fact . . . that in making critical references to the work of my contemporary authors I try as a rule to compare them to the real masterpieces. . . . Nor perhaps, seeing him as I did as the Fortunate Youth with a nimbus of glory, did I sympathize with his 'disasters' as others may have done."— Quoted in David Harvey, *Ford Madox Ford 1873-1939* (Princeton, N. J., 1962), pp. 234-35.

[17] Ford, *Return to Yesterday*, p. 29.

And no matter how attractive Crane's personality seemed to Ford, he always returned to the important point that Crane was primarily an artist, a poet. He might be other-worldly, but he observed minutely. He might sustain a *persona* of defiant harshness, but he craved praise for his writing. Like the other English authors who knew Crane, Ford loved Crane for his combination of courage and frailty, generosity and poverty, pride and misfortune; yet Ford "revered" Crane because he was "such a beautiful genius."[18] To Ford, Crane was a serious man of letters. Crane gained admiration for his achievement as a "distinguished human being."[19] He was, Ford insisted, a poet because "no more poetic view of humanity in our late Armageddon was ever written than the *Red Badge of Courage.*"[20]

Ford's own work aimed at clarity, design, economy, and *progression d'effet;* the author who would write in *The Good Soldier* what is called the most perfect French novel in English, whose early heroes were Turgenev and Flaubert, saw in Stephen Crane's fiction a complete break from the sprawling tradition

[18] *Ibid.,* p. 49. Crane's "natural character," said Ford, was that of "a singularly refined and studious human being."— "Stevie and Co.," p. 24. In his review of Beer's *Life,* Ford rejected the view of Crane as a roisterer and Bowery tough. "Actually, Crane was a very normal and sensible citizen of the Republic of Letters."—"Stevie," *New York Post Literary Review* (July 12, 1924), 881.

[19] Ford, *Mightier Than the Sword,* p. 46.

[20] Ford, *Return to Yesterday,* p. 63.

of the English novel. He found in Crane's writing the conscious stylistic control that Ford, Conrad, and James strove for against the main stream of English fiction. The collaboration of Ford and Conrad aimed at combining *le mot juste* with the ideal structure. And, as Allen Tate put it, "Ford believed passionately in the novel as a work of art, a distinct *genre* to be explored and developed in terms of form, not of social ideas or mere subject matter."[21] Stephen Crane shifted his primary allegiance from Howells (social ideas) and Garland (subject matter) to Ford and other English writers because Crane himself was becoming increasingly interested in the art of the novel. It was fitting that one of his strongest supporters should be a writer who became distinguished for careful control and selective technique. To Ford, Crane shared with Conrad a passion for elisions, "for cutting his phrases down to an almost infinite economy of words. He was never tired of exasperatedly declaring that it was his unattainable ambition to make every one damned word do the work of six."[22] In the Butler Library Crane Collection is a note written on a telegraph blank "And His Name Shall Be Called Under Truth/ Because He Said Far Less Than He Was Able."

Stephen Crane would often comment to Ford on the excesses of others. Ford frequently quoted Crane

[21] "Homage," pp. 487-88.
[22] Ford, "Techniques," p. 26.

58

on Robert Louis Stevenson: "I remember hearing him . . . comment on a sentence by Robert Louis Stevenson that he was reading. The sentence was: 'With interjected finger he delayed the motion of the timepiece.' 'By God, poor dear!' Crane exclaimed. 'That man put back the clock of fiction fifty years.' "[23] This remark may not have been, as Ford elsewhere claimed, the most profound remark about English prose that he ever heard.[24] Nevertheless, Ford continued to insist that Crane was fascinated by diction. " . . . I used to listen for hours whilst Stephen Crane talked just about words!"[25]

While neither Ford nor Crane could absolutely be trusted on the matter of Crane's knowledge of French authors, Ford was accurate in his opinion that Crane's formulae were similar to those of the "Flaubert-Maupassant-Turgenev school."[26] Ford recalled Crane's conversations about trips that he wanted to take not as referring to the places themselves but to the places as possible subjects for his rendering in prose. "He talked, in fact, about his technique."[27] Ford summarized his impression of

[23] Ford Madox Ford, *Memories and Impressions* (London, 1911), p. 58.

[24] Ford Madox Ford, *Thus To Revisit* (London, 1921), p. 69.

[25] *Ibid.*, p. 69.

[26] *Ibid.*, p. 110.

[27] *Ibid.*, p. 109. One of Crane's rare statements about the craft of fiction appeared in "War Memories" when he described a Cuban church that was being used as a hospital. After an impressionistic passage, Crane commented, "I bring this to you

59

Crane's view of writing in a trenchant phrase: "He possessed, in fact, in a remarkable degree not only the Literary Gift but the Literary Sense—and a devouring passion for words."[28]

Ford never wrote an actual review or strict piece of criticism about Crane's writing; the praise for Crane's fiction was scattered impressionistically throughout Ford's publications. He was steadily convinced of the realism—the realism that went beyond the Civil War and applied to all wars—of *The Red Badge of Courage*. "When I was at the Front, on Kemmell Hill in 1916, I had . . . the curious experience of so reading myself into the *Red Badge of Courage* which is a story of the American Civil War, that, having to put the book down and go out of my tent at dawn, I could not understand why the men I saw about were in khaki and not in the Federal grey."[29] (This last word was a Ford slip, one which he corrected to "blue" in subsequent versions.) Just how well Ford appreciated Crane's war stories

---

merely as an effect, an effect of mental light and shade, if you like; something done in thought similar to that which the French impressionists do in color; something meaningless and at the same time overwhelming, crushing, monstrous." Note that even here Crane was more inclined to use terms of reference drawn from painting than fiction ("War Memories," in *The Work of Stephen Crane*, IX, 246).

28 Ford, *Thus to Revisit*, p. 111.

29 Ford, *Return to Yesterday*, p. 49. Ford re-read *Youth, Heart of Darkness,* and *What Maisie Knew* just before this. Cf. Harvey, *Ford Madox Ford*, p. 234.

can be seen by the technique of describing men in battle in *Parade's End*—which followed Crane's map that showed them their own hearts.[30] Ford wrote

[30] Ford, *Mightier Than the Sword*, p. 40. Ford's own view of war, recaptured in two volumes of his tetralogy *Parade's End*— *No More Parades* and *A Man Could Stand Up* (1925, 1926)— reflected his personal experiences of World War I and the more general conditions of trench warfare that a generation of British soldier-authors treated in memoirs and novels. Edmund Blunden, Siegfried Sassoon, Richard Aldington, Robert Graves, among many other writers, paralleled Ford's combination of disgust at war's horror and grudging pride in the protagonist's ability to withstand the terrors. Ford's war fiction does seem to owe something to *The Red Badge of Courage*. Like Crane, Ford showed men advancing in a body despite their individual fears: "All moving towards places towards which they desperately don't want to go. Desperately! Every one of them is desperately afraid. But they go on."—*Parade's End* (New York, 1950), p. 453. The impressionism that distinguished Crane's war novel was one of Ford's fundamental techniques. As a recent critic has said, " . . . in his last books, he was even to employ some of the flashing imagery that in modern writing ultimately derives from Crane."—John Meixner, *Ford Madox Ford's Novels* (Minneapolis, Minn., 1962), p. 24. In passages of battlefield description, Ford, like Crane, used rapidly fleeting details and sharply contrasting colors: "Miles and miles away to the left . . . beneath the haze of light that, on a clouded day, the sea threw off, a shaft of sunlight fell, and was reflected in a grey blur. . . . It was the glass roofs of a great airplane shelter. A great plane, the largest he had then seen, was moving over, behind his back, with four little planes as an escort. . . . Over the vast slagheaps by Béthune. . . . High, purplish-blue heaps, like the steam domes of engines or the breasts of women. . . . Bluish-purple" (*Parade's End*, p. 493). Ford's hero feels curiosity and fear, learns the mysteries of heroism, mourns for a dead comrade— whose demise matches that of Crane's Jim Conklin—and understands, like the narrator of "War Memories," the value of the veteran: "The man had fired with care, had come down to reload with exact drill movements—which are the quickest possible" (p. 581). As Ford put it, "I should not be surprised if it could

61

Conrad highly praising "The Price of the Harness" upon its publication.[31] *The Open Boat* collection was, according to Ford, "the finest volume of true short stories in the English language";[32] "The Five White Mice" was "one of the major short stories of the world."[33] Crane's subjects were properly the men in outposts of progress, the wagers of ridiculous little wars whom he nailed "down in his impressions as few other lives have been nailed down."[34]

Ford and Conrad shared an enthusiasm for Crane's phrase from "The Open Boat," "the waves were barbarous and abrupt [sic—actually, 'most wrongfully and barbarously abrupt']." And Ford stressed consistently, clearly, and emphatically the idea that Stephen Crane, Joseph Conrad, Henry James, and, by implication, Ford Madox Ford were all laborers together in the vineyards of the new novel, the novel of selection as Henry James would call it, contrasting it to the novel of saturation as practiced by, ironically enough, Crane's other great supporter, H. G. Wells. In the nineties, said Ford, there were three names

be revealed to me that when I was lately writing about the emotions of the trenches I was influenced—and very profoundly— by Stevie's rendering of the emotions of a man gazing into a gun barrel."—"Stevie and Co.," p. 30.

[31] Conrad to Crane, January 13, 1899, Stallman and Gilkes (eds.), *Letters,* p. 205.

[32] Ford, *Memories and Impressions,* p. 58.

[33] Ford, "Techniques," p. 32.

[34] Ford, *Mightier Than the Sword,* p. 268.

of importance for the student of the English novel—James, Crane, and Conrad.[35] "About that . . . triad there was a certain solidarity, a certain oneness of method and even a certain comradeship. They lived in the same corner of England, saw each other often and *discussed literary methods* more thoroughly and more frequently than can ever at any other time in England have been the case."[36] "I discussed literary problems and their personal techniques . . . with Crane and Hudson . . . and others. . . . "[37] Even though Wells could jest about this group of foreigners plotting against the traditional English novel,[38] the three authors did have similar credos. James and Conrad articulated their philosophies of the novel in letters, prefaces, and reviews; Ford was sure that Crane shared the opinions the other two made explicit. They all subscribed to Conrad's dictum in the preface to *The Nigger of the Narcissus* that the

35 Ford Madox Ford, *The English Novel* (Philadelphia, 1929), p. 142.

36 Ford, *The English Novel*, p. 143 (my italics). Ford's statement is supported by fuller examples than some of his more impressionistic judgments receive and has the ring of truth. Elsewhere he called the three "almost equally, the protagonists of literary Impressionism in Anglo-Saxondom. . . . " —"Techniques," p. 26. Again, "That literary nook of England which centered around Rye and which held Conrad, Crane, and Henry James, all living in a singularly close communion, was a decent and respectable nook of honest men who . . . had the same purity of aim . . . and their methods were all kindred. . . . "—"Stevie and Co.," p. 24-25.

37 Ford, "Techniques," p. 32.

38 Ford, *The English Novel*, p. 143.

63

novelist's first duty was to make the reader see: " . . . and Crane might have written the same thing had he ever written about himself."[39]

Conrad, Crane, and James—all exiles, all separated from the popular literary groupings, the decadents, the jingoists, the compilers of family chronicles. With Ford they tried to render rather than tell, to exhaust all possible effects, to remain objective, to avoid the device of the intrusive author, to write about what they knew—in other words, to define and achieve a technique. These three, along with W. H. Hudson and sometimes Wells and John Galsworthy, were interested in form. They were not moralistic, Ford held; indeed, he never heard Crane come forth with any moral platitude.[40] They all wrote in very concrete terms of the human condition. Ford remembered "Stevie" scoffing at English literature as a silly parlor game that only treated of tea-parties and flimsy adventures. Thus, Ford clearly realized that Crane differed from his fellow authors in subject-matter. He wrote of physical life, wars, slums, saloons. James wrote of teas, Conrad wrote of wars and teas. If Crane's work was dominated by the revolver, Conrad's was less so; if James's work was dominated by moral scruple, Conrad's was equally less so. But Crane and Conrad both were looking for the figure in the carpet. The three writers shared the same

[39] *Ibid.*, p. 145.
[40] Ford, *Mightier Than the Sword*, p. 267.

64

literary method: " . . . The approach to life is the same with all these three: they show you that disillusionment is to be found alike at the tea-table, in the slum, and on the tented field."[41] The three exiles and the Englishman all sought to force the reader to assert, "I have been in a drawing room overlooking Boston Common, in a drinking saloon in Yellow Sky, or beneath the palm leaves of Palembong."[42]

As Ford Madox Ford made clear throughout his discussions of Stephen Crane, while he attracted warm friends by virtue of his personality that was at once warm, colorful, and gallant, he built up intellectual acceptance on the parts of these writers by his sharing in their artistic credos. They worked for the same stylistic effects, had the same fundamental themes, were held together by their commitments to craft. Ford understood Stephen Crane's artistry. Crane was the equal in intent and partial achievement of Henry James and Joseph Conrad.

[41] Ford, *Return to Yesterday*, p. 217.
[42] Ford, *The English Novel*, p. 145.

5

FORD MADOX FORD HIMSELF WAS NOT sure of the nature of the relationship between Stephen Crane, who could fall into crude Bowery postures, and Henry James, who could insist on fastidious Anglicized reticences. Realizing the surface absurdity of an intellectual rapport between the two, Ford nevertheless insisted that there was a close companionship. Crane had "a deep reverence and a great affection for the master. . . . " and "that James had a very great admiration for Crane I know. He constantly alluded to Crane as 'that genius,' and I have heard him say over and over again, 'He has great, great genius. . . .' "[1] Although Ford probably embroidered the story that James sought to buoy up the dying Crane's spirits with New England delicacies purchased from Wanamakers, the truth behind the anecdote remained. James did suffer "infinitely for the dying boy"; and, probably, "he was

[1] Ford, "Stevie and Co." pp. 24, 26.

67

not himself for many days after Crane's death."[2] But Ford could not finally understand the link that joined the two authors. Crane apparently showed respect and enthusiasm for James's works. Ford, however, felt that the talk of James and Crane was usually superficial, even though Ford did attest that he heard them talk about each other often when the other was not present. What was the common experience that the two novelists shared?[3] The answer lay in professional and artistic realms.

Since both Crane and James would assume masks and often present different faces to different audiences, it is difficult to trust the statements of those who observed their meetings. Crane's niece remembered his using an East Side accent at will, talking with brewery drivers or with Theodore Roosevelt in appropriate phrases.[4] James could be different to different men: he bored Hugh Walpole, fascinated Arthur Benson, seemed spiteful to Sidney Colvin, appeared warm and sympathetic to A. C. Bradley.[5] Yet these two novelists, two Americans wrapped in

[2] Ford, *Return to Yesterday*, p. 31.

[3] A guest who stayed with the Cranes often at Brede from July to January, 1899, stated that Crane paid frequent visits to Rye, and James bicycled over to Brede every week (Edith R. Jones, "Stephen Crane at Brede," *Atlantic Monthly*, CXCIV [July, 1954], 57).

[4] Helen R. Crane, "My Uncle Stephen Crane," *American Mercury*, XXXI (January, 1934), 26.

[5] *The Legend of the Master*, ed. Simon Nowell-Smith (London, 1947), p. xliii.

Sussex sea mist, as one of their acquaintances put it,[6] were close friends. James once brought a carriage load of people to lunch at Brede; he sponsored Cora's admission to the Mermaid Club, was photographed eating a doughnut at Cora's lawn party.[7] Crane told James tales of boxers, brandished a revolver, rescued his top hat from a drunken woman.[8]

That the relationship went beyond surface friend-liness was made clear by James's reaction to his young compatriot's fatal illness. James not only cabled to America for food, he also rushed to London to seek a specialist for the dying man. This reaction was partly a product of what Crane had called James's obvious kindness—" . . . it seems impossible to dis-like him. He is so kind to everybody . . . "[9] —and partly James's protective feeling toward his younger companion: "One day Mr. James and Stephen were having a discussion about something, and Stephen was getting the better of the argument. Suddenly Mr. James said, 'How old are you?' 'Twenty-seven,' said Stephen. 'Humph,' said Mr. James, 'prattling babe!' "[10] James sent Cora Crane fifty pounds to aid the sick man; money, he said, that "meagrely repre-

[6] Claire Sheridan, *Nuda Veritas* (London, 1927), p. 29.

[7] Lillian Gilkes, *Cora Crane* (Bloomington, Ind., 1960), pp. 122, 204, 205.

[8] Thomas Beer, "Stephen, Henry, and the Hat," *Vanity Fair* (August, 1922), p. 63.

[9] Beer, *Stephen Crane,* p. 170.

[10] Jones, "Stephen Crane at Brede," p. 57.

sents my tender benedictions to him."[11] A few days after Crane's untimely death, James surveyed the empty Brede Place and discovered it to look conscious and cruel. That day he wrote to H. G. Wells, "You will have felt, as I have done, the miserable sadness of poor Crane's so precipitated and, somehow, so unnecessary extinction."[12]

There remained vast differences in the subject matter, the approaches to fiction of these two novelists. How could the mild, peaceful Henry James understand and appreciate Crane's tales of violence? Why would James be drawn to *The Red Badge of Courage* in particular? For the answer, we need only to peruse James's autobiographical writings.

Perhaps the least noticed aspect of Henry James's mind is his fascination with the Civil War. Biographers have struggled with the problem of James's injury, physical or psychical, that kept him out of the war and forced him to remain an observer, to live inwardly rather than to serve actively as did his brothers Robertson and Wilky. Unlike Oliver Wendell Holmes, Henry James never had his heart touched by fire through active participation in the "whole air of life and sharp experience."[13] But the

11 Gilkes, *Cora Crane*, p. 254. Miss Gilkes has discovered no documentation to support John Berryman's story that James said, "I've money, and moreover I care."

12 *Henry James and H. G. Wells*, ed. Leon Edel and Gordon N. Ray (London, 1958), p. 68.

13 Henry James, *Notes of a Son and Brother*, in *Autobiography*, ed. Frederick W. Dupee (London, 1956), p. 460.

amount of space James gave to the descriptions of military engagements, heroic youths, bitter tragedies, underlined his fascination with the facts and emotions of the soldier's life that he never led.

Over fifty years after the Civil War, Henry James, using letters and family documents, provided in *Notes of a Son and Brother* a magnificently lyrical view of the details and emotional overtones of the conflict. He set forth brief elegies of the dead: Will Temple, radiant and gallant, killed at Chancellorsville in 1863 (the battle described by Crane in *The Red Badge of Courage*); Robert Gould Shaw, wounded in the attack on Fort Wagner. Like a patriotic Harvard professor who saw himself as the guardian of sacrificed young men, James considered that "certain of them whom I had neither seen nor, as they fell in battle, was destined ever to see, have lived for me since as communicated images. . . . "[14] Vicarious pity and wonder were all James was allowed to feel, to his infinite and pervasive regret. "I had, under stress, to content myself with knowing it in a more indirect and muffled fashion than might easily have been. . . . All of which, none the less, was not to prevent the whole quite indescribably intensified time . . . from remaining with me as a more constituted and sustained act of living, in proportion to my powers and opportunities than any other homogene-

14 *Ibid.,* pp. 428-29.

ous stretch of experience that my memory now recovers."[15]

Hating to miss the "outwardness" of military experience, James became one of the earliest Civil War buffs. He felt a part of the national consciousness of crisis, regretted that *he* would not be up and doing, and compensated by getting deeply involved, as a patriot, in the fate of the Northern armies. During the war years, James avidly kept in touch with military news, often visited camps and hospitals. He saw the wounded in their tents at Portsmouth Grove, Rhode Island, and described them in emotional, almost Whitmanesque terms.[16] The young James achieved "visionary 'assistance' at the drama of the War" by visiting the Forty-fourth Massachusetts Regiment at camp in Readville. He found the regiment to be luminous and beautiful, while the Fifty-fourth Massachusetts, a Negro regiment, seemed "sinister and sad."[17] Always these visits were undercut by a sense of envy and deprivation brought on by his younger brothers' military initiations.

James's identification with the soldiers on active duty was immediate and powerful. We can under-

[15] *Ibid.*, pp. 382-83.

[16] He spoke of his first sight of the Northern soldier as equal in effect to the "tender, elegiac tone in which Walt Whitman was later on so admirably to commemorate him." James listened to the stories of the wounded and gave them money "like dear old Walt—even if I hadn't come armed like him with oranges and peppermints."—*Ibid.*, pp. 422, 424.

[17] *Ibid.*, pp. 456-57.

72

stand James's sense of excitement when, in 1895, he read Crane's re-creation of the war that could still cause a vicarious thrill when James reread his brother's letters in 1914. "When I read again . . . that 'Sherman leaves tonight from Beaufort with Logan's Corps . . . ' the stir as of great things rises again for me, wraps about Sherman's name as with the huge hum that then surrounded it, and in short makes me give the passage such honour as I may. 'We are waiting anxiously for the sound of his musketry announcing him.' I was never in my life to wait for any such sound, but *how* at that juncture I hung about with the privileged Wilky!"[18]

As James's memories of the war remained intense and his sense of missed opportunities was always acute, so his emotion of animation, of romantic stimulation, continued to mark his memories of those fortunate enough to go to war. The soldiers, albeit sometimes amusing and rueful, were figures of romance.[19] In their companies and regiments, these uniformed heroes achieved a sense of community and an understanding of America that would elude James as he sought to rediscover his country in *The American Scene*. Here he would look at statues of Sherman, graveyards in Richmond, and agree with Mark Twain about the huge fallacy of the Southern idea, the vanity and fatuity of the

[18] *Ibid.*, p. 470.
[19] *Ibid.*, p. 424.

73

Confederate dream.[20] As he thought of his youth, however, James remembered his uncritical idealizations of the Northern soldier. When Henry James knew him, Stephen Crane in "War Memories" was idealizing the regulars of the Spanish-American War in terms remarkably similar to those James was to employ in his reminiscences of the Civil War volunteers. James, in "blue horizons," saw "laughing, welcoming, sunburnt young men . . . and who had all alike turned handsome . . . under I couldn't have said what common grace of clear blue toggery. . . . "[21] An outsider, James missed, as he was often to miss, the great opportunity for vision, *"the appreciation of the thing* seen."[22] How well, then, would James understand Crane's drive to prove the truth of *his* vision of war, to experience for himself the events described in his war novel—by going to the wars in Greece and Cuba—to gain an appreciation of the thing seen. If Crane was realistic in his fiction, he was romantic in his fascination with war. And Henry James was also. When another great war occurred in 1914, H. G. Wells would treat the war in *Mr. Britling Sees it Through,* Ford Madox Ford

[20] Henry James, *The American Scene* (New York, 1946), pp. 371, 373.

[21] James, *Notes,* p. 456. Compare Crane's description of "each hard bronzed profile" who had "the grace of a man whose rifle has become absolutely a part of himself."—*The Work of Stephen Crane,* IX, 23.

[22] James, *Notes,* p. 460.

would volunteer, although fat and over-age, for active duty—which he would recapture in his finest fiction. James would still be unable to live by his eyes; at best he could take out British citizenship. In 1914, however, he could remember how as a youth he, like Stephen Crane, longed to be chasing the wars.

When the Civil War ended and the armies came home, James felt overwhelmed by images of military experience. It was literally brought home to him, by the matured faces and characters of his countrymen, the enormous "absolutely acquired and stored resources of overwhelming reference"[23] that he had missed. James recalled the very smell of having served, the masculine communication that Crane made the subject matter for most of his fiction. Even old, worn-out uniforms seemed dramatic to James. Unlike Crane, unlike Conrad, James was never "one of us." "It had been unprecedented at least among ourselves; we had had it, in our own highly original conditions— or 'they' to be more exact, had had it admirably in theirs; and I think I was never to know a case in which his having been directly touched by it, or in a word, having consistently 'soldiered,' learnt all about it and exhausted it, wasn't to count all the while on behalf of the happy man for one's own individual impression or attention."[24] Need one necessarily wonder what Henry James, snugly ensconced in Rye,

[23] *Ibid.*, p. 488.
[24] *Ibid.*, p. 489.

75

and Stephen Crane, recently returned from the Cuban wars, would have to discuss? Indeed, in an essay on the fiction of Harold Frederic, Crane mentioned the Civil War in language similar to that of James. Frederic, said Crane, wrote of "the great country back of the line of fight—the waiting women, the lightless windows, the tables set for three instead of five—was a land elate or forlorn, triumphant or despairing, always strained, eager, listening, tragic in attitude, trembling and quivering like a vast mass of nerves from the shock of the far away conflicts in the South. These were supreme years. . . ."[25]

Henry James wrote three "Civil War stories" early in his career, "The Story of a Year" (1865), "Poor Richard" (1867), and "A Most Extraordinary Case" (1868). Although none of the stories treat of combat, all three present central characters who have been shattered by the war. Like the hero of "The Story of a Year," these figures bring into the peaceful North "some of the reality of war,—a little whiff of gunpowder, the clanking of a sword."[26] In this story Jack Ford imagines war in lush, romantic terms that sound like Henry Fleming's early dreams of battle. "There were columns charging and columns flying and standards floating,—tatters of reflected purple; and great captains on colossal horses, and a rolling

[25] Crane, "Harold Frederic," pp. 358-59.
[26] *The Complete Tales of Henry James,* ed. Leon Edel (London, 1962), I, 49.

canopy of cannon-smoke and fire and blood. The background of the clouds, indeed, was like a land on fire, or a battle-ground illumined by another sunset, a country of blackened villages and crimsoned pastures."[27] James, like Thackeray in *Vanity Fair*, does not follow the hero to war; the author remains behind with the civilians. "I have no intention of following Lieutenant Ford to the seat of war. The exploits of his campaign are recorded in the public journals of the day, where the curious may still peruse them."[28] Thackeray could not describe war because he was a "non-combatant"; James evidently shared these scruples, despite his belief that the subject matter for fiction need not be drawn from direct experience.[29] James's question, "Who can tell the story of those red months?"[30] was later answered by the young Stephen Crane.

When the young man in James's story is seriously wounded (like James's brother), the heroine (like James himself?) feels left out of the main stream of life. "In emergencies, such persons are tacitly counted out; and they as tacitly consent to the arrangement."[31]

[27] *Ibid.*, I, 51.

[28] *Ibid.*, I. 67.

[29] In "The Art of Fiction," James spoke directly to this point: "The young lady living in a village has only to be a damsel upon whom nothing is lost to make it quite unfair (as it seems to me) to declare to her that she shall have nothing to say about the military."—*The Future of the Novel*, ed. Leon Edel (New York, 1956), p. 12.

[30] *The Complete Tales*, I, 67.

[31] *Ibid.*, I, 76.

"Poor Richard" also showed a wounded officer who, in this case, after recovery goes back to war and is killed by a guerrila. Once again James indicated war's horror through the words of a character who is forced merely to observe: "War is an infamy, Major, though it *is* your trade. It's very well for you, who look at it professionally, and for those who go and fight; but it's a miserable business for those who stay at home, and do the thinking and the—the *missing!*"[32] Yet, the Civil War gives the weakling of the title an opportunity for redemption through going to war and purging himself of guilt by suffering the pains of active service. In "A Most Extraordinary Case," still another wounded soldier comes home to die of his war injuries. The narrator of the tale analyzes the officer's three years of arduous duty in terms that seem to reveal James's sense of guilt at missing the war more clearly than does any statement in his later autobiographical writings. "On the few occasions when he had been absent from the scene of his military duties, although duly authorized and warranted in the act, he had suffered so acutely from the apprehension that something was happening, or was about to happen (some chance for distinction, some augmentation of honour), which not to have witnessed or to have had a hand in would be matter of eternal regret that he can be barely said to have

[32] *Ibid.,* I, 241.

78

enjoyed his recreation."[33] The whole Civil War, as represented obliquely, fleetingly, in Henry James's youthful fiction, gave him a "sense of lost time"[34] that would make him understand and, indeed, admire Stephen Crane's attempts to seize for himself and fix in his art the facts of war.

Although over three decades passed from the time of the Civil War to the time that James met Crane, James never lost his interest in war, not only the Civil War that he treated fully in his memoirs, but European wars as well. According to Leon Edel, "The Civil War letters of his brothers form a logical bridge to Henry's later reading of war memoirs and Napoleonic lore. The passionate interest with which he absorbed the three volumes of Marbot in the 1890's represented a continuation of the earlier experience . . . he continued over the years to read other war letters, and the passages he marked in Marbot are not unlike those he excerpted from Wilky's letters— scenes of violence, storming of positions, the rugged life and observations of men committed to action."[35] With such a continuing interest, James must have appreciated Stephen Crane's fictional version of war, also stimulated by the reading of memoirs and by

[33] *Ibid.*, I, 331. These last two stories were in Stephen Crane's library.

[34] *Ibid.*, I, 331.

[35] Leon Edel, *Henry James: The Untried Years* (Philadelphia, 1953), p. 188.

sheer imagination. Moreover, James would be impressed by Crane's deep concern for getting his characters and situations right, a concern that drove Crane to leave the peaceful Surrey hills and to follow scenes of violence. As James put it, "My relation to Crane was—I am happy in thinking—unblemished in cordiality. The difference in our ranges of habit and experience was terrific. He had many admirable qualities, but he had lived with violence."[36]

In the 1890's, James also wrote about the nature of military courage and cowardice in "Owen Wingrave," a "pacifist" story which describes the moral force that leads a young man to refuse military service despite his family's long tradition of soldierly honor. Owen Wingrave's quiet, isolated courage allows him to spend a night's vigil in a haunted room; this vigil brings about his death—on his own chosen battlefield. In his notebook entry for May 8, 1892, James wrote, "Can't I hammer out a little the idea—for a short tale—of the young soldier?—the young fellow who, though predestined, by every tradition of his race, to the profession of arms, has an insurmountable hatred of it—of the *bloody* side of it, the suffering, the ugliness, the cruelty; so that he determines to reject it for himself. . . ."[37]

[36] Beer, "Stephen, Henry, and the Hat," p. 63.
[37] *The Notebooks of Henry James*, ed. F. O. Matthiessen and Kenneth B. Murdock (New York, 1955), p. 119.

80

Henry James would understand Crane's need to prove his combat courage in Greece and Cuba. Unlike James, Crane had dared to write about a great war in which he had not served. Henry James could admire Crane's moral courage in writing the novel James never attempted, in using the materials of the Civil War in fiction. What James had to talk about with the Crane who returned to England fresh from the Cuban battlefields should be quite clear from the tone of James's letter to Field Marshal Viscount Wolsely who sent James the two volumes of the *Story of a Soldier's Life* in 1903.[38] "To a poor worm of peace and quiet like me—yet with some intelligence—the interest of communicating so with the military temper and type is irresistible—of getting so close (comparatively!) to the qualities that make the brilliant man of action. Those are the qualities, unlike one's own, that are romantic, that you have lived all your days by and with them and for them, I feel as if I had never questioned you nor sounded you enough. . . . I would give all I have (including Lamb House) for an hour of your retrospective consciousness, one of your more crowded memories—that for instance of your watch, before your quarters, during the big fight in Ashantee. . . ."[39]

[38] Edel, *Henry James*, p. 187.

[39] Quoted in Edmund Wilson, *Patriotic Gore* (New York, 1962), p. 663.

In a review of Thomas Beer's life of Stephen Crane, Ralph Paine, an old newspaperman and friend of Crane during his filibustering days, expressed astonishment at the Crane-James friendship. "Never was there an odder association than that between the vagabondish young Crane, lawless of convention, startling of speech, despising all else than the naked truth, and the elderly novelist who had become a colored and complicated ritual. . . . "[40] Paine continued to ask why James "could send the weary young impressionist five manuscripts unasked and request an opinion of them"—a story reported only in Beer, by the way. We must ask the same question: How could Crane, a wretched speller, a professedly rapid writer, help with James's careful, almost tortured, prose? Crane refused to rewrite *The Third Violet* because it had already been published in one version; he felt that such rewriting would be "dishonest."[41] Crane never kept a Jamesian notebook, wrote an introduction, nor (after his second novel) employed the painter's sponge. Speaking of Eugene Field, Crane asserted, early in his career, that a

[40] Ralph Paine, "The Life and Art of Stephen Crane," *Bookman* (New York), LVIII (December 23, 1923), 471.

[41] John Berryman, *Stephen Crane* (New York, 1950), p. 142. But Willa Cather remembered Crane's stressing the time he took to work up detail: " 'The detail of a thing has to filter through my blood, and then it comes out like a native product, but it takes forever.' "—Willa Cather, "When I Knew Stephen Crane," *Prairie Schooner*, XXIII (Fall, 1949), 235. (Reprinted from *Library,* [June 23, 1900]).

82

writer should not concern himself with superficial matters of culture, but should concentrate on an understanding of man, especially the American western man, and not have anything to do with an "adoration for effete jugs and old kettles."[42] (The comment by Crane came two years before James wrote *The Spoils of Poynton!*) Certainly the two men displayed many dissimilarities in personality, style, and approach. Yet, at the start of Crane's short career, James defended *The Red Badge of Courage* to the skeptical Harold Frederic,[43] and at the end James complained bitterly of the useless extinction. To James, Crane's death was "an unmitigated, unredeemed, catastrophe." James was particularly disturbed by the loss of Crane's *"possibilities* and *powers."*[44]

Clearly James would not have reacted in this fashion at the death of an author without great potential; and Crane was growing in literary knowledge and sensibility to the end of his life. Much of this growth came through James. Beer described James quoting Gide to Crane while Crane told James how cowboys lived—and how good an Anatole France story was.[45] In 1899, Crane received a copy of James's

[42] Letter to Willis Hawkins, November 5, 1895, Stallman and Gilkes (eds.), *Letters,* p. 69.

[43] Beer, *Stephen Crane,* p. 137.

[44] Gilkes, *Cora Crane,* p. 262 (my italics).

[45] Beer, *Stephen Crane,* p. 244.

short novel *In the Cage,* elaborately and affectionately inscribed.[46] Crane was bored by the novel, just as he had been by James's *The Reverberator,* felt that the girl did not think directly enough, but liked the middle chapters, after James really got started.[47] Crane thought *The Portrait of a Lady* was a masterpiece.[48] (He was "ardent" about the novel and understood how James avoided the preaching that annoyed Crane in Tolstoy's *Anna Karenina*).[49] And Crane wrote in the *Bookman,* in 1898, about *What Maisie Knew*: "Mr. James' book is alive with all the art which is at the command of that great workman."[50] Crane read not only James's fiction but also some of his criticism—particularly on French authors. As early as 1895, Stephen Crane was ready to think seriously about critical problems raised by James and to take issue with the master. "What, though, does the man mean by disinterested contemplation? It won't wash. If you care enough about a thing to study it, you are interested. . . . It clamours in my skull that there is no such thing as disinterested contemplation, except that empty-as-a-beerpail look

[46] *Ibid.,* p. 224.

[47] Berryman, *Stephen Crane,* p. 237.

[48] Beer, *Stephen Crane,* p. 166.

[49] Berryman, *Stephen Crane,* p. 183.

[50] Crane, "Concerning the English 'Academy,'" p. 23. In the Crane Collection in the Butler Library of seventy-five books owned by Stephen or Cora are four by Henry James, *The Bostonians, The Spoils of Poynton,* and *Stories Revived* (First and Second Series).

84

that a babe turns on you and shrivels you to grass with. Does anybody know how a child thinks?"[51] The problem that James carefully worked out in *What Maisie Knew* and "The Pupil" was to engage Crane's final literary efforts, the brilliant tales of childhood that made up his *Whilomville Stories.* Like James, a frustrated dramatist; like James, a severe critic of journalists (compare *The Reverberator* with the ironic passages of *Active Service* or *The Third Violet*); like James, able to judge and reject Mrs. Humphry Ward's work—which pained James and forced Crane to consider *Robert Elsmere* "higgling rubbish"[52]—in the final analysis, like James, Crane was perfectly capable of discussing the art of fiction. We may trust Beer's avowal that at a party Crane and James went off in a corner to talk *style.* Crane wrote almost no criticism; but when he did, it made sense. He understood the limitations of Ouida and Harold Frederic. He clearly realized that *Under Two Flags* was "a thing of imperfect creation"; although in what was almost a puff, he admitted to a nostalgia for the novel's sentiments.[53] In an article on Frederic for the *Chap-Book,* Crane praised the realistic stories of the Mohawk Valley and perceived the falling-off in Frederic's English stories which were excessively

[51] Beer, *Stephen Crane,* p. 147.

[52] Berryman, *Stephen Crane,* p. 74.

[53] Stephen Crane, "Ouida's Masterpiece," *Book Buyer,* XIII (January, 1897), 969.

reports of the author's personality.[54] He saw the strength of early Wells novels such as *Kipps* and *Mr. Polly* and anticipated Wells's later weakness. "I should say that Mr. Wells will write better and better when he sticks to character altogether and does not concern himself with narrative."[55] Like Henry James, Stephen Crane called for form and control. Thomas Hardy was a gigantic writer who overtreated his subjects; Mark Twain's novels were too long. Surely James would have echoed Crane's decision that "Four hundred pages of humour is a little bit too much for me."[56] Despite his belief that Tolstoy was the supreme writer of Crane's time, he had to "confess that the conclusions of some of his novels, and the lectures he sticks in, leave me feeling that he regards his genius as the means to an end. I happen to be a preacher's son, but that heredity does not preclude— in me—a liking for sermons unmixed with other material. . . . I mean that I like my art straight."[57]

Both John Berryman and Daniel Hoffman have argued for similarities between Crane and James;

[54] Crane, "Harold Frederic," pp. 358-59.

[55] Beer, *Stephen Crane,* p. 244. And James liked Wells's stories because his characters were "so alive and kicking."— Edith Wharton, *A Backward Glance* (New York, 1934), p. 181.

[56] Berryman, *Stephen Crane,* p. 249.

[57] Beer, "Introduction," to *The Work of Stephen Crane,* VII, xiii. Elsewhere Beer speaks of Crane's "quick sympathy with Mr. Shakespeare," and his understanding of the "fine quality" of Hamlet despite the ugliness of Polonius' death and the treatment of the Queen ("Five Feathers," *Saturday Review of Literature,* II [December 19, 1925], 426).

86

the one found that the authors shared a definition of the novel as a direct impression of life and sought an intensity of this impression; the other joined these two writers of the nineties in their acceptance of the autonomy of art.[58] Like James, Crane realized that art was an effort born of pain. If James wrote of the growth from innocence to experience in "The Pupil," *The Portrait of a Lady,* and *The Wings of the Dove,* for example, so did Crane, perhaps with less subtlety, in "The Open Boat" and *The Red Badge of Courage.* They both wrote many tales of writers and artists, and in these both skirted the basic questions involved in describing the creative process. The two men wrote of the heartbreak of childhood, of the need for moral decisions. The terror of *The Turn of the Screw* was paralleled in miniature by Crane's little-known "An Illusion in Red and White." James probed society in *The Princess Casamassima,* Crane rejected society in *The Monster.* To be sure, Crane was violent where

[58] Berryman, *Stephen Crane,* p. 55; Hoffman, *The Poetry of Stephen Crane,* p. 240. Ray B. West, Jr., has recently argued for a similarity between "The Bride Comes to Yellow Sky" and *The American*: " . . . We must say that it is the tale of a childlike man confronting a new, and more complex, situation than his simple code allows for. Scratchy Wilson differs only in degree from James' Christopher Newman."—"Stephen Crane: Author in Transition," *American Literature,* XXXIV (May, 1962), 222. See also Thomas A. Gullason, "The Jamesian Motif in Stephen Crane's Last Novels," *Personalist,* XLII (Winter, 1961), 79: " . . . The aristocratic Henry James, a close friend in his last years . . . gave Crane the incentive . . . to deal more probingly with the problem of class against class, as James had done so successfully."

James was restrained, Crane was sketchy where James was exhaustive. The differences were immense, but similarities of form and content were also evident. Both experimented with point of view. Both avoided fully detailed plots, completely delineated characters. Both were misunderstood by contemporary reviewers and accused of the same so-called faults, faults that the twentieth-century critic, having developed an acceptance of complexity and a taste for the difficult, would call perfections. To the *Athenaeum* reviewer, Crane's stories seemed to be "studies in narrative, rather than narratives told for the sake of the stories themselves; thus there is always something a little artificial about them."[59] Reviewers accused Crane and James alike of the sin of not presenting complete works. Crane was reprimanded for being more interested in the manner in which an event came to pass than in the event itself, for choosing slight incidents rather than dramatic events. Referring to *The Third Violet*, a reviewer was quite explicit: "In his present book Mr. Crane is more the rival of Mr. Henry James than Mr. Rudyard Kipling."[60] And Joseph Conrad asserted that James considered *The Third Violet* to be the piece of Crane's work that represented "the right thing."[61]

[59] *Athenaeum* (March 16, 1901), 334.

[60] *Athenaeum* (May 22, 1897), 618.

[61] Thomas Beer, "The Princess Far Away," *Saturday Review of Literature*, I (April 25, 1925), 702. Ford Madox Ford shared James's high opinion of the novel's "marvelous economy."— "Stevie and Co.," p. 28.

Certainly we must show great care in an examination of the basis for the friendship between Stephen Crane and Henry James. The evidence is meager. In all James's correspondence there is no direct reference to Crane's fiction.[62] The dissimilarities are obvious. At best we can only conjecture that Crane understood and admired James's approach to fiction because the younger man was attempting, in his way and with superficially different materials, to create similar tough, enigmatic challenges to the reader's intelligence. We can also conjecture that James appreciated Crane's attempts and that James would have spoken of Crane as of Howells: " . . . With the most distinguished dexterity and all the detachment of a master, he handles some of the clumsiest, most human things in life."[63] Unlike Henry James, however, Joseph Conrad had a friendship with Crane that left no room for doubt or conjecture. The mutual respect between Crane and Conrad was obviously based on art as well as personality.

[62] Leon Edel, in a letter to the author, February 20, 1962.

[63] James, "Introduction," to Rudyard Kipling, *Soldiers Three* (Leipzig, 1891), p. xii.

89

6

IN *WAR IS KIND,* CRANE OUTLINED THE nature of his friendship with Joseph Conrad:

> There was a man with tongue of wood
> Who essayed to sing,
> And in truth it was lamentable.
> But there was one who heard
> The clip-clapper of this tongue of wood
> And knew what the man
> Wished to sing,
> And with that the singer was content.

Without doubt Joseph Conrad loved Stephen Crane as a person; Conrad also understood the younger man's artistic integrity and achievement. Crane returned the understanding.

As Conrad wrote many times, it was an admiration for each other's work that brought the two authors together in England, the older man as eager to meet

Crane—who was the senior as an author—as the younger was to meet the author of *The Nigger of the Narcissus*. The key to the basis for their relationship appeared in the circumstances of this first meeting. Although Crane gave the initial impetus by asking Sidney Pawling, his publisher, to provide the introductions, Conrad was highly flattered that the author of *The Red Badge of Courage* wanted to see him. The mutual attraction was based on their work, even before the London luncheon with Pawling and Crane, "I *do* admire him. I shan't have to pretend."[1] The admiration was to deepen into a permanent friendship. James Gibbons Huneker, years after Crane's death, noticed Crane's photograph on Conrad's desk as a testimony to the strength of Conrad's love.[2]

That Joseph Conrad was the one who heard "and knew what the man / Wished to sing" became clear in Conrad's essays on Crane's work. In his introduction to Beer's *Life,* Conrad hit on the essential fact about Crane's war novel—that it dealt with the relations of the individual to the group, that the story belonged as much to the regiment as to the young soldier—a fact that almost no other critic noticed. Because of the performance in *The Red Badge of Courage,* Conrad was sure that Crane would under-

[1] Conrad to Garnett, October 14, 1897, Garnett (ed.), *Letters from Joseph Conrad,* p. 115.

[2] James Gibbons Huneker, *Steeplejack* (New York, 1921), II, 128.

stand *The Nigger of the Narcissus,* the book that remained Conrad's favorite among his works. And Crane did understand. During their long first day spent wandering through the streets and parks of London, he warmed Conrad's heart by saying, "'I like your young man—I can just see him,'" in response to Conrad's "'I like your general.'"[3] They met as novelists; they expressed their knowledge of each other's conscious mastery of the art form by picking for praise, in Conrad's words, the merest by-the-way vignette of a minor character. "It was the meeting of 'The Red Badge' and 'The Nigger.'"[4]

The friendship developed and strengthened from this first meeting of minds to a final permanent loyalty. Two months later, the men sat up half the night at Conrad's house, smoking and talking.[5] Crane and Conrad lived nearby in order to share views of life and art; they went on vacation together; and they talked of sharing a house, collaborating on a play, buying a boat. It was Conrad who helped to finance Crane's trip to Cuba by borrowing from a publisher. And it was Conrad who kept Crane's memory alive in the early years of the twentieth century by continuing to pay homage to his work. Although he told Garnett that the introduction to Beer's life of Crane was written with some reluctance be-

[3] Conrad, "Stephen Crane," pp. 322-23.

[4] *Ibid.,* p. 318.

[5] Conrad to Garnett, December 5, 1897, Garnett (ed.), *Letters from Joseph Conrad,* p. 118.

93

cause he did not like to feed on the memory of his friends,[6] he insisted that he was pleased to pay tribute to the memory of his intimate for whom he had both great admiration and affection.[7]

One of Conrad's friends has pointed out that he sought as companions persons who were not necessarily intellectual but whose outlooks agreed with his own.[8] Crane's "intense earnestness," his "delicacy of sentiment," his being "incapable of affection" attached him to Conrad;[9] " . . . there were profound, if not extensive, similitudes in our temperaments."[10] Mrs. Conrad attested to the young American's gifts and charm. She was pleased by the "easy terms of complete understanding" that existed between Crane and her husband.[11] Conrad appreciated Crane not only as a man of action—a type, according to John Galsworthy, that Conrad had great regard for[12]—but primarily as a deeply sensitive, brooding visionary who shared Conrad's heart of darkness.[13] Conrad

[6] Conrad to Garnett, March 10, 1923, ibid., p. 291.

[7] G. Jean-Aubry, Joseph Conrad, Life and Letters (London, 1927), I, 297, 302.

[8] Richard Curle, The Personality of Joseph Conrad (London, n.d.), pp. 8-9.

[9] Conrad, "Stephen Crane," pp. 318-19.

[10] Ibid., p. 338.

[11] Jessie Conrad, "Recollections of Stephen Crane," Bookman (New York), LXII (April, 1926), 134.

[12] John Galsworthy, Two Essays on Conrad (Privately printed, 1930), p. 54.

[13] Joseph Conrad, "Stephen Crane: A Note without Dates," Bookman (New York), L (February, 1920), 529.

always insisted that the relationship between the two was one of respect as well as love. His inscription in Crane's copy of *Almayer's Folly* put into words this consideration: "To Stephen Crane, with the greatest regard and most sincere admiration."[14] William Rothenstein described Conrad's rejection of most English authors and acceptance of French writers; he reserved warmth and respect mainly for James and Crane.[15] To Crane, Conrad could say in reference to *The Nigger of the Narcissus,* "You at any rate will understand and therefore I write to you as though we had been born together before the beginning of things."[16]

The much more reticent Stephen Crane found in Joseph Conrad the literary friend he had been seeking all his life. Crane needed the personal support he got from the Conrads, who took Crane and his wife into their home, exchanged visits,[17] found money when needed, and let Crane, who loved children, play with their son. He needed, as Mrs. Conrad said, "the admiration each artist had for the other, and

14 Carl Bohnenberger and Norman Mitchell Hill (eds.), "The Letters of Joseph Conrad to Stephen and Cora Crane," *Bookman* (New York), LXIX (May, 1929), 227.

15 William Rothenstein, *Men and Memories* (London, 1938), III, 28.

16 Conrad to Crane, November 16, 1897, Stallman and Gilkes (eds.), *Letters,* p. 151.

17 "We spent ten days with Stephen Crane and his wife at Ravensbrook."—Jessie Conrad, *Joseph Conrad as I Knew Him* (New York, 1926), p. 44.

that something akin in each personality that made their friendship a thing apart."[18] Even more than personal warmth—which, after all, he received from Harold Frederic—Crane needed an adviser, a literary man to respect. He wanted praise for what he was trying to do, praise from competent writers; at this stage in his career Garland and Howells were of no help. They were in America, and they still believed that *Maggie, George's Mother,* and the "Midnight Sketches" were Crane's best work. A writer, Crane insisted, needed support from a fellow-practitioner who could tell whether or not he was making an advance in his work.[19] This "Polish friend . . . who is an unancient mariner"[20] helped to answer to Crane's intellectual and emotional needs. Huneker thought that Crane spoke of Conrad as the devout speak of the Virgin Mary.[21] And if Conrad remained loyal to the Cranes, Crane returned the loyalty. On his deathbed, Crane asked Sanford Bennett to use pressure in order to get Conrad placed on the Civil List.[22] Conrad was the only man with whom Stephen Crane could possibly entertain the thought of collabo-

[18] Jessie Conrad, "Recollections," p. 135.

[19] Crane to William Crane, October 24, 1897, Stallman and Gilkes (eds.), *Letters,* p. 146.

[20] Beer, *Stephen Crane,* p. 194.

[21] *Ibid.,* p. 219.

[22] Crane to Sanford Bennett, May 29, 1900, Stallman and Gilkes (eds.), *Letters,* p. 284.

rating; he would share a meal, an evening, a house, or a writing assignment with his friend.

In his understanding of the quality of Crane's genius, Conrad did not close his eyes to the weakness in Crane's makeup that challenged the eventual fulfilment of this genius. He knew the limitations of Crane's knowledge; as Conrad said to Cunninghame Graham, however, " . . . The man after all knows something."[23] And if Crane had no critical small talk, neither did Conrad. "I must confess that we were no critics, I mean temperamentally. Crane was even less of a critic than myself." But Conrad went on to undercut this statement. "Criticism is very much a matter of vocabulary, very consciously used; with us it was the intonation that mattered. The tone of a grunt could convey an infinity of meaning between us."[24] Conrad was able to measure how little Crane had seen of the world at large in comparison to Conrad's own wide experience, but he also understood how much Crane's imaginative grasp of facts, events, and men could make up for this limited view. Similarly, Conrad granted Crane's equally limited knowledge of literature; once more Conrad felt certain that it did not affect the quality of Crane's style.[25]

Despite his apologies for Crane's weaknesses, Joseph Conrad was too honest a man not to entertain

[23] Jean-Aubry, *Joseph Conrad,* I, 230.
[24] Conrad, "Stephen Crane," p. 332.
[25] Conrad, "A Note without Dates," p. 530.

doubts. He saw the disorganized Crane household in all its confusion. He listened to his editor who insisted that there was no justification for Crane's unstable temperament and confused financial state.[26] Early in his career, Crane himself questioned whether he was using all the eloquence and intelligence he had at his disposal. When Conrad knew him, Crane was desperately writing against time, turning out the same kind of hack work, on occasion, that another expatriate novelist, F. Scott Fitzgerald, would pour forth a generation later. Knowing the depth of Crane's own doubts ("He is strangely hopeless about himself"[27]), Conrad feared, in 1897, that Crane might not go as far as he should. It was only a feeling, not a considered opinion. Yet, when he closed Crane's war novel, Conrad felt vaguely uneasy, as if Crane's mastery could only last while one was caught up in the act of reading, as if Crane had no staying power. To their common friend Garnett, Conrad unburdened himself of these doubts in an extremely revealing letter: "His grip is strong but while you feel the pressure on your flesh you slip out from his hand—much to your own surprise. That is my stupid impression and I give it to you in confidence."[28]

[26] Joseph Conrad, Letters to William Blackwood and David S. Meldrum, ed. William Blackburn (Durham, N. C., 1958), p. 20.

[27] Conrad to Garnett, December 5, 1897, Garnett (ed.), Letters from Joseph Conrad, p. 118.

[28] Loc. cit.

Crane could not remain popular unless he could move beyond simple strength, rapid action, and amazing vision. In other words, Crane needed a more mature point of view. Looking back, Conrad understood that Crane was only half aware of his abilities. The older author was willing to mourn his young friend's death as a personal loss; but unlike James, Conrad did not think that Crane's death represented a loss to literature, " . . . for I think he had given his measure fully in the few books he had the time to write."[29] While Conrad had his doubts about Crane's future work, they were largely based upon the instability of Crane's temperament. Conrad's assessments of Crane's body of work leave little room for doubt.

Stephen Crane himself considered Joseph Conrad to be the finest writer of his generation. It was because he liked *The Nigger of the Narcissus* that he sought Conrad out, and Conrad always appreciated the fact that his new friend was fit to pronounce judgment on this early effort. And Crane widely pronounced these judgments. In response to his rapturous praise of the novel, which he called "a crackerjack,"[30] Hamlin Garland had to confess that he lacked knowledge of Conrad's work[31] and asked

[29] Conrad, "A Note without Dates," p. 530.

[30] Gilkes, *Cora Crane*, p. 126.

[31] Bohnenberger and Hill (eds.), "Letters of Joseph Conrad," p. 227.

for a copy of the book. Crane told Huneker that Conrad was writing the most wonderful stories in English.[32] Crane tried to persuade an American publisher, Irving Bacheller, to get Conrad's novel serialized.[33] The young American novelist also praised Conrad in print. In his 1898 *Bookman* piece, Crane took exception to critics who called *The Nigger of the Narcissus* "episodic," a critical term that he found worthless. (This by way of comment on Garnett's criticism of *The Red Badge of Courage?*) The article left no question as to Crane's evaluation: " . . . his novel is a marvel of fine descriptive writing. It is unquestionably the best story of the sea written by a man now alive, and as a matter of fact, one would have to make an extreme search among the tombs before he who has done better could be found. . . . He comes nearer to an ownership of the mysterious life on the ocean than anyone who has written in this century."[34] Coming from the man who wrote "The Open Boat," the praise meant a great deal to Conrad, so much so that he was unwilling to review *The Open Boat* volume for fear that he would be accused of log-rolling. Tempted, Conrad heeded his qualms: "The excellent fellow in the goodness of his heart has been praising me beyond my merits on his own side of the water and his generous utterances

[32] Huneker, *Steeplejack,* II, 128.

[33] Crane to Conrad, November 11, 1897, Stallman and Gilkes (eds.), *Letters,* p. 150.

[34] Crane, "Concerning the English 'Academy,' " p. 23.

have been quoted here. . . . Consequently my review would do no good to Crane's work, which deserves a warm appreciation."[35]

Crane was willing to express his opinion of the novel directly to Conrad and wrote him that the book was "simply great." Crane was particularly impressed by Conrad's simple, yet detailed treatment of Wait's death. "By such small means does the real writer suddenly flash out in the sky."[36] Conrad responded warmly to this appreciation. "When I feel depressed about it I say to myself 'Crane likes the damned thing'—and am greatly consoled."[37]

In letters, articles, introductions, and memoirs, Joseph Conrad continued faithfully to acclaim Stephen Crane's accomplishment in fiction. Conrad steadily supported his fellow-novelist when he wondered about the value of his work. Often, as in the case of Crane's volume of poetry *The Black Riders*, Conrad would restrict his appreciation to a few words and an approving grunt.[38] Conrad was accustomed to reading Crane's stories in manuscript and in proof, to talking all night about form and content. After the works were published, Conrad took every opportunity to express his understanding of Crane's attempts. In 1897, Conrad wrote Crane to tell him

[35] Jean-Aubry, *Joseph Conrad*, I, 231.

[36] Crane to Conrad, November 11, 1897, Stallman and Gilkes (eds.), *Letters*, p. 150.

[37] Conrad to Crane, December 1, 1897, *ibid.*, p. 154.

[38] Conrad, "Stephen Crane," p. 331.

that "A Man and—Some Others" was "great." " . . . I admire it without reserve. It is an amazing bit of biography."[39] Conrad encouraged Crane to write what would be one of his finest and most mature works, *The Monster*—which had haunted Conrad ever since the other writer outlined his plans for the tale.[40] In 1899, Conrad mentioned his delight in the mellowness and vigor of "The Price of the Harness."[41] (Of this story he had written to Cora Crane a month earlier, "His story . . . is magnificent. . . . He is maturing. He is expanding. There is more breadth and somehow more substance in this war picture. . . . There is an added ampleness in his method which makes me augur a magnificent future for his coming work."[42]) Perhaps Conrad's fullest indication of Crane's success came in an early letter that praised *The Open Boat* book: "I am envious of you—horribly. Confound you—you fill the blamed landscape—you—by all the devils—fill the sea-scape. The boat thing is immensely interesting. I don't use the word in its common sense. It is fundamentally interesting to me. Your temperament makes old things new and new things amazing. . . . You are an everlasting surprise to one. You shock—and the next moment you give the perfect artistic satisfaction.

[39] Conrad to Crane, December 1, 1897, Stallman and Gilkes (eds.), *Letters*, p. 154.

[40] Conrad to Crane, January 16, 1898, *ibid.*, p. 169.

[41] Conrad to Crane, January 13, 1899, *ibid.*, p. 205.

[42] Conrad to Cora Crane, December 4, 1898, *ibid.*, p. 197.

Your method is fascinating. You are a complete impressionist. The illusions of life come out of your hand without a flaw. It is not life—which nobody wants—it is art."[43] One can imagine the satisfaction the letter must have afforded Stephen Crane.

What Conrad wrote to Crane was passed on to others. Conrad told Edward Garnett a few days later that while both stories were excellent, and "A Man and—Some Others" was the better story, "The Open Boat" interested him more.[44] To Garnett, he sustained this opinion of Crane's work twenty-four years later in agreeing about the value of the war pieces. "They are good. And truly in all the work he left behind him there is nothing that could be dismissed as rubbish."[45] Conrad's loyalty led him to repeat his enthusiasm for "The Price of the Harness" to William Blackwood. Pointing out a satisfaction with the story and a firm belief that Crane would do even better work in the future, Conrad held that the tale was "broader, gentler, less tricky and just as individual as the best of his work. It is the best bit of work he had done since the *Red Badge*."[46]

[43] Conrad to Crane, December 1, 1897, *ibid.*, p. 154.

[44] Conrad to Garnett, December 5, 1897, Garnett (ed.), *Letters from Joseph Conrad*, p. 118.

[45] Conrad to Garnett, January 17, 1921, *ibid.*, p. 276.

[46] Conrad to William Blackwood, December 13, 1898, Blackburn (ed.), *Letters to William Blackwood*, p. 34. Said Ford, "I can still remember the frantic admiration, the *shouts* of joy, he [Conrad] uttered whilst just reading 'The Four [sic] White Mice.' "—Ford, "Stevie and Co.," p. 30.

103

In his formal essays on Crane's work, Conrad naturally concentrated on *The Red Badge of Courage,* the book that he urged on Cunninghame Graham late in 1898.[47] In his preface to the novel, later collected in Conrad's essays under the title of "His War Book," he stressed Crane's inspired gift for rendering the significant surface details and for delving into primitive emotions.[48] Conrad attested to the permanence of Crane's picture of a young, untried man caught in a situation that was beyond his comprehension. The modernity of Crane's novel was proved by World War I, said Conrad. The small gem of a novel was concerned with elemental truth; thus, as an artist, Crane stood alone—"He dealt with what is enduring, and was the most detached of men."[49] In reference to "The Open Boat," Conrad wrote of the "inspired audacity of epithet" in "that marvelous story . . . which by the deep and simple humanity of presentation seems somehow to illustrate the essentials of life itself, like a simple tale."[50] More generally, Conrad wrote eloquently of Crane's earnestness of purpose, comprehension of the tragic issues of life, and forceful and imaginative style.[51] If, as Mrs. Conrad held, both men benefited from the inter-

[47] Jean-Aubry, *Joseph Conrad,* I, 220.
[48] Conrad, "His War Book," p. 343.
[49] *Ibid.,* p. 346.
[50] Conrad, "Stephen Crane," p. 324.
[51] Conrad, "A Note without Dates," p. 529.

change of ideas,[52] if, as Conrad himself stated, Crane "had a wonderful power of vision which he applied to the things of this earth and of our mortal humanity,"[53] then the explanation for the mutual sympathy between the two novelists in all probability lay in the similarities to be found in their fiction.

Publishers and reviewers were accustomed to lumping the two names together. "I was so glad you could meet Crane and Conrad—the two foremost of the youngest [sic] writers just now. . . . "[54] The review by Arthur Quiller-Couch in the *Pall Mall Magazine* of *The Nigger of the Narcissus* praised it for having some of Mr. Crane's insistence,[55] while the *Speaker* made Conrad's novel, in its vividness and fulness of detail, a worthy pendant to the battle pictures of *The Red Badge of Courage*.[56] As Conrad wrote Cunninghame Graham, "There are twenty years of life, six months of scribbling in that book—and not a shadow of a story. As the critic in today's *D'ly Mail* puts it tersely: 'The tale is no tale at all' [a familiar complaint in the reviews of Crane's stories]. The man complains of lack of heroism [the problem of *The Red Badge of Courage*] and is, I fancy, shocked at

[52] Jessie Conrad, "Recollections of Stephen Crane," p. 136.

[53] Conrad, "A Note without Dates," p. 529.

[54] Meldrum to Blackwood, March 26, 1898, Blackburn (ed.), *Letters to William Blackwood*, p. 20.

[55] *Pall Mall Magazine*, XIV (January 15, 1898), 425.

[56] *Speaker*, XVII (January 15, 1898), 83.

the bad language"[57] (as were the reviewers of *Maggie* and *George's Mother*). Two days later, Conrad was seriously disturbed by a review of his novel in the *Daily Telegraph,* written by its regular reviewer, W. L. Courtney. Conrad wrote Crane, "I may be a little fool but I know better than to try to imitate the inimitable. But here it is. Courtney says it. You are a lost sinner and you have led me astray. If it was true I would be well content to follow you, but it isn't true."[58]

Conrad's note of asperity was justified by the review. In the discussion of *The Nigger of the Narcissus* that appeared in the *Daily Telegraph,* W. L. Courtney echoed the *Daily Mail* and complained about Conrad's excessive technique, which served to bury the "story." The passages in the article that mentioned Crane were condescending in tone and made Conrad a deliberate imitator of the younger author. "Mr. Joseph Conrad has chosen Mr. Stephen Crane for his example, and has determined to do for the sea and the sailor what his predecessor had done for war and warriors. The style, though a good deal better than Mr. Crane's, has the same jerky and spasmodic quality; while a spirit of faithful and minute description—even to the verge of the wearisome—is common to both." Courtney went on to describe the

[57] Jean-Aubry, *Joseph Conrad,* I, 212.

[58] Conrad to Crane, December 24, 1897, Stallman and Gilkes (eds.), *Letters,* p. 157.

novel in terms that might very well be applied to "The Open Boat," and ended his piece with a further attack on Conrad's short, staccato sentences: "It is in these that the example of Mr. Crane is most obvious and potent upon him."[59] It is interesting to remark that two years earlier Courtney was responsible for one of the negative reviews of *The Red Badge of Courage*. This review employed the same terms that Courtney later applied to Conrad's book; the critic rejected Crane's lack of story, found the spasmodic style to be crude.[60]

For all Conrad's pique with the enforced connection to Crane, Conrad realized the similarities in their approaches to their work. When Crane proposed to Conrad that the two men collaborate on a play, Conrad was tempted by the idea, for "there were profound, if not extensive, similitudes in our temperaments which could create for a moment that fascinating illusion."[61] The play itself, as Crane conceived it, turned on the idea of a man impersonating his dead "predecessor" in the attempt to win the love of a beautiful girl. Looking back on the proposed drama —which the two would often discuss but never start— Conrad saw the idea as fairly ridiculous, bound to be melodramatic, and manifestly impossible to stage. (Crane wanted the man and the girl to appear stand-

[59] *Daily Telegraph* (December 8, 1897), p. 7.
[60] *Daily Telegraph* (November 29, 1895), p. 7.
[61] Conrad, "Stephen Crane," p. 338.

107

ing by their dead ponies on an open plain after a wild ride into the sunset. Conrad admitted that the scene might have been effective in a film.) The idea of the play, which was to be called "The Predecessor," died hard with Crane. In January, 1898, Conrad wrote to his friend, expressing an unwillingness to collaborate, and insisted that Crane, depending on his own clear eye, terse style, and easy imagination, go it alone. "You want no help. I have a perfect confidence in your power." Yet, Conrad went on, he would be willing to see an outline and perhaps to work by Crane's side and under Crane's direction. "And *quién sabe?* Something perhaps would get itself shaped to be mangled by the scorn or the praise of the Philistines."[62] A few weeks later, Crane was still after Conrad. "He won't believe me when I swear by all the gods and all the muses that I have no dramatic gift. Probably something will be attempted but I would bet nothing shall be done."[63] The idea of the project dribbled to nothingness, despite Crane's appeal to Garnett to approve the collaboration. Garnett, while sufficiently moved by Crane's infectious enthusiasm so as to raise no objections, understood Conrad's skepticism.

Nevertheless, thirteen years later, Conrad employed Crane's idea in the short story "The Planter

[62] Conrad to Crane, January 12 [?], 1898, Stallman and Gilkes (eds.), *Letters*, p. 167.

[63] Jean-Aubry, *Joseph Conrad*, I, 228.

of Malata." Despite a change in the setting and characters, the story of unrequited passion and the nature of truth and lies had a vague echo of Crane, as did the hero, a lean, lounging man. Conrad wondered whether or not Crane would be pleased with the tale if he were able to read it over Conrad's shoulder: " . . . Perhaps, after picking up the volume with that detached air I remember so well and turning over page after page in silence, he would suddenly read aloud a line or two and then, looking straight into my eyes as was his wont on such occasions, say with all the intense earnestness of affection that was in him: 'I—like—that, Joseph.' "[64]

The two writers never officially collaborated, but their similarities in style and content made the concept viable in the eyes of reviewers and of the men themselves. What were these similarities?

Both Joseph Conrad and Stephen Crane sought organic structure for their fiction, tried to follow Flaubert in using the precise phrase, worked to *render* a story rather than simply tell it, struggled to make ordinary language fresh and suggestive. Both authors stressed the technique of implying much more than they stated, of presenting the effect of an event on character. It was this power of suggestion that most critics misunderstood when they accused Crane and Conrad, ironically enough, of lacking substance simply because much was left unsaid. (As Crane once

[64] Conrad, "Stephen Crane," p. 340.

109

stated to a journalist, " . . . whether I say a thing or suggest it, I try to put it in the most forcible way."[65] What distinguished the fictional approach of Crane and Conrad from that of the majority of their contemporaries was the delicacy, the subtlety, the ironies of the two authors' tales of action and adventure. Like Robert Louis Stevenson, they wrote of men of action; but like Henry James, they concentrated on manners and motives—of these men of action. Conrad's MacWhirrs and Bakers acted; his Marlows and Jims contemplated action. In the same way Crane's Flemings and Collinses acted; his Easterners and Dr. Trescotts questioned the motives of action. Both authors wrote of the weakness and cowardice of men. In the worlds of violence created by Conrad and Crane, the essential tension derived from this conflict between action and inaction, between physical description and analysis of feeling.

The two men were equally impressionists, presenting the outside of events—wars, murders, shipwrecks —and implying from the direct impression of life the wonder and mystery of human endeavor. In other words, Crane and Conrad (like James) concentrated on intensity of atmosphere as a way of indicating ideas rather than directly expressing them. H. E. Bates has commented on the fact that Crane shared

[65] Harold P. Williams, "Mr. Crane as a Literary Artist," *Illustrated American* (July 18, 1896), p. 126.

110

with Conrad "a genius for creating a peculiar intensity of atmosphere."[66] As Conrad wrote Galsworthy, in 1898, in reference to the latter's most recent work, "the force of the book is in the fidelity to the surface of life, to the surface of events—to the surface of things and ideas. Now this is not being shallow."[67] And when Conrad and Crane discussed fiction, they considered it in terms of craft, not of abstractions or philosophies. What T. S. Eliot has written of Henry James in another context applied equally well to Crane and Conrad whose critical genius also came out in their mastery over and "baffling escape from, Ideas, a mastery and an escape which are perhaps the last test of a superior intelligence."[68] This control of the surface led both writers to a dependence on careful verbal technique: irony and symbolism provided the structure of their works from *The Nigger of the Narcissus* and *The Red Badge of Courage* through *Nostromo* and *The Monster*. Crane obviously understood the need for formal control, as obviously as did Conrad or James. Writing about Harold Frederic, Crane pontificated, "There are writing men who, in some stories, dash over three miles at a headlong pace, and in an adjacent story move like a boat over ploughed fields; but in Frederic one feels at once the

[66] Bates, "Stephen Crane," p. 11.

[67] Jean-Aubry, *Joseph Conrad,* I, 224.

[68] T. S. Eliot, "On Henry James," in *The Question of Henry James,* ed. F. W. Dupee (London, 1947), p. 125.

perfect evenness of craft, the undeviating worth of the workmanship. . . . "[69]

Like many other novelists, Crane, Conrad, and James all needed only a hint or a brief experience to give them a theme for their imaginative explorations of men's acts. For James, an anecdote at the dinner table was sufficient; for Conrad, one short landing in his youth at a South American port led years later to *Nostromo*; for Crane, an overnight stop in a western hotel gave setting and theme of "The Blue Hotel." Unlike James, however, Crane and Conrad were also accustomed to using their immediate experience, as in *Youth* and "The Open Boat," for some of their best work. Again, Crane was as interested as were Conrad and Ford in problems of time manipulation, seeking simultaneity and foreshortening in nearly all of his tightly packed short novels and stories.

Most English and American writers of the 1890's wrote novels either of sensation (exciting plots, exotic settings) or saturation (naturalistic piling up of powerful detail, realistic collection of ordinary events). Henry James and Ford Madox Ford, like some continental authors, wrote novels of sensibility (character nuances in minutely described settings) and selection

[69] Crane, "Harold Frederic," p. 359. And Crane was sensitive to the structural demands of a book of short stories. He realized that while "Death and the Child" would not fit in the same volume with *The Monster*, "The Blue Hotel" would (Allen, *Paul Revere Reynolds*, p. 57).

(carefully chosen, often symbolic details, rare action). Crane and Conrad combined the best of both worlds and wrote fiction of selection and sensation. In their novels and stories, violent action took place in wildly adventurous settings—in African jungles and Texan plains. Still, Crane and Conrad never accepted life at the expense of form nor form at the expense of vitality. Like Conrad, Crane at his very best made experience and imagination coalesce into the superb artistic transmutation of "The Open Boat" and "The Blue Hotel," and, also like Conrad, he often flawed the attempted combination in his longer, more romantic, novels.

The subject matter that attracted the two novelists was remarkably similar, and called for the joining of sensational scenes with subtle characterizations. As Crane and Conrad wrote of the moral dilemmas that faced men trying to live according to a code, they treated, with uncompromising realism and acute observation, the intense situations that tested men's spirits. Conrad employed, to be sure, a more meditative style and worked technical marvels in his manipulation of point of view and time shifts, but both discussed the difficulties of acting in moments of stress, difficulties that made the shadow line between courage and cowardice dim indeed. Their sensitive heroes, Lord Jim and Henry Fleming, for example, often failed these tests and had to work out their guilt under conditions of bitter isolation. Some, like

Fleming and the Marlow of "The Heart of Darkness," succeeded; others, like Decoud in *Nostromo* and Peza in "Death and the Child," failed. And sometimes, as in "Amy Foster" and *The Monster,* the failure was ghastly in its horror. The relations of individuals to the group were probed in such works as "The Blue Hotel" and *Under Western Eyes;* an individual's response to pressure in "The Secret Sharer" and "A Mystery of Heroism," both of which stories turned on a similar existential conception of the gratuitous act that imposed conditions of danger in order to temper the spirit. The authors drew characters without roots who were types rather than fully rounded personalities.

What H. E. Bates has said about Crane fitted Conrad equally well: the two writers were at their best in describing primitive emotions of fear, anger, hatred, jealousy, terror.[70] They used similar settings. The sea in many of their stories was the backdrop for the ultimate pressures that make or break men; *Typhoon* and "The Open Boat," *Youth* and "Flanagan's Short Filibustering Adventure" showed the sea as both friend and foe to man. Although Crane was the great chronicler of men at war, Conrad in a number of stories, "Gasper Ruiz," "The Duel," "The Warrior's Soul," described the suffering of the retreat of Napoleon's armies from Moscow or the misery of South American revolutions. Crane's "The Clan of

[70] Bates, "Stephen Crane," p. 11.

114

No Name" and Conrad's *Nostromo* alike revealed the terms of guerrilla death. No matter what the setting, nature was predominantly hostile, or at least indifferent. Conrad was fascinated by Crane's overwhelming picture of nature's refusal to pity man in "The Open Boat." Conrad spoke of the story in terms that recalled Stein's famous advice to Lord Jim to sink himself in the destructive element and by the exertions of his hands keep himself afloat. Conrad said that he and Crane felt "how uncertain was the issue of life envisaged as a deadly adventure in which we were both engaged like two men trying to keep afloat in a small boat."[71] And then Conrad quoted to Crane his lines describing nature's lack of sympathy, " 'None of them knew the colour of the sky.' " Conrad himself in the story "Initiation" treated the sea in an identical manner. As the crew of a sinking Danish ship leaped into lifeboats, their clatter "had an extraordinarily destructive effect upon the illusion of tragic dignity our self-esteem had thrown over the contests of mankind with the sea. . . . The cynical indifference of the sea to the merits of human suffering and courage . . . revolted me."[72] So Crane's correspond-

[71] Conrad, "Stephen Crane," p. 324.

[72] Joseph Conrad, "Initiation," in *The Mirror of the Sea* (London, 1906), p. 223. Late in his life, Henry James was to write of his fears of World War I, " . . . The huge shining indifference of Nature strikes a child to the heart and makes me wonder of what abysmal mystery, or villainy indeed, such a cruel simile is the expression."—*The Selected Letters of Henry James,* ed. Leon Edel (New York, 1960), p. 215.

115

ent cursed the seven mad gods who would not respect his efforts. Finally, neither author was successful in his frequently attempted portraits of women; theirs were men's worlds.

Conrad and Crane examined fine consciences, then, in isolation or in relation to society. While writing about individuals, the authors universalized and treated the ironies and fears of mankind. As Carl Bohnenberger brilliantly put it, "A man with the greatest power of observation and a consummate knowledge of mankind, with a clarity of vision that had come from the sea, Conrad cared for men in the many ways that his greatness allowed him to see them. Before Stephen Crane everything fell away and was vanquished in the art and humanity in which each was supreme. The Crane who wrote of Yankee soldiers and of desolate human beings, plucked out of the rude mass of America, understood the mind that created Almayer, the symbol of tragic hope, and Peter Willems, the child of despair; and was understood."[73]

The idea of Stephen Crane, the inarticulate, attractive, immature, lucky journalist who fell upon a society of fellow authors as fortunately as he discovered happy metaphors and blundered upon appropriate structural devices—this image was false. Obviously, Crane's English friends, from Edward Garnett and Ford Madox Ford to H. G. Wells,

[73] Bohnenberger and Hill (eds.), "Letters of Joseph Conrad," p. 228.

Henry James, and Joseph Conrad, respected not only the man's powerful personality that was at once appealing and tragic but also—and especially—Crane's understanding of, and interest in, the problems raised by the craft of fiction, problems that he solved brilliantly and entirely self-consciously in his own work, which was the product of an incisive and serious intellect.

Stephen Crane's short life came to an end after a series of hemorrhages which followed his first attack during a Christmas houseparty at Brede Place at the close of 1899; Wells, Ford, James, and Conrad were present at this first intimation of Crane's mortality. He died in Germany on June 5, 1900, after having worked up to the end of his career on his *Whilomville Stories* and on the unfinished *The O'Ruddy* (probably completed by Robert Barr). To consider Crane an expatriate writer may seem extreme; he spent only from September, 1897, to April, 1898, and then from January, 1899, to June, 1900, in England—about two years. Yet these two years represented a large part of Stephen Crane's adult writing span. Furthermore, much of his life outside England was spent collecting experiences that went into his fiction; the Bowery nights, the Greek adventures, the Caribbean shipwrecks, and the Cuban battles, all were recollected in the tranquillity of Surrey.

Weak efforts like *Active Service* and *The O'Ruddy* appeared in England, to be sure. Much of Crane's best work, however, was written or first published in

England. There he wrote his brilliant short stories, at once realistic and enigmatic, "The Bride Comes to Yellow Sky," "The Blue Hotel," "Death and the Child," "A Man and—Some Others," "The Five White Mice," "The Price of the Harness," and his four brief, mordant war stories, in the Biercean manner, about the Kicking Twelfth. And in England, Crane wrote his two finest books—after *Maggie* and *The Red Badge of Courage*—the horrifying social satire *The Monster* and the ironic and nostalgic stories of childhood, *Whilomville Stories*. Accompanying his friendships with serious novelists like James and Conrad was a steady growth in Crane's own art, in control of his irony, in dark vision, and in intense selectivity. His years in England and the fruitful friendships with England's best novelists might have led Stephen Crane to produce a canon of fiction that would compete with the achievements of his peers, Joseph Conrad and Henry James. Instead, Crane's early death forced the entire output of his art to be as selective and foreshortened, as brief and as doubtful, and, finally, as ironic as his own finest individual stories and novels. As one of his English obituaries put it, "To his friends he was known as 'Steve.' Of a bright, boyish disposition, under a pale and delicate exterior was the heart of the young 'lion.' He held his own life and reputation cheaply [but was] a rising hope."[74]

[74] *Evening News* (June 5, 1900), p. 13.

Bibliography

Bibliography

ALLEN, FREDRICK LEWIS. *Paul Revere Reynolds.* New York, 1944.

ALLEN, JOHN BARROW. Review of *The Red Badge of Courage, Academy,* Vol. XLIX (February 15, 1896).

BATES, H. E. *Edward Garnett.* London, 1950.

————. "Stephen Crane: A Neglected Genius," *Bookman* (London), Vol. LXXXI (October, 1931).

BEER, THOMAS. "Five Feathers," *Saturday Review of Literature,* Vol. II (December 19, 1925).

————. Introduction to *The Work of Stephen Crane,* ed. WILSON FOLLETT. Vols. VI, VII. New York, 1926.

————. "The Princess Far Away," *Saturday Review of Literature,* Vol. I (April 25, 1925).

————. *Stephen Crane.* London, 1924.

————. "Stephen, Henry, and the Hat," *Vanity Fair,* August, 1922.

BERGONZI, BERNARD. *The Early H. G. Wells.* Manchester, England, 1961.

BERRYMAN, JOHN. *Stephen Crane.* New York, 1950.

BOHNENBERGER, CARL, and HILL, NORMAN MITCHELL (eds.), "The Letters of Joseph Conrad to Stephen and Cora Crane," *Bookman* (New York), Vol. LXIX (May, June, 1929).

BROOKS, SIDNEY. "Stephen Crane and the Critics," *Dial,* Vol. XX (May 16, 1896).

CADY, EDWIN. *Stephen Crane.* New York, 1962.

CATHER, WILLA. "When I Knew Stephen Crane," *Prairie Schooner,* Vol. XXIII (Fall, 1949). Reprinted from *Library,* June 23, 1900.

CONRAD, JESSIE. *Joseph Conrad and His Circle.* London, 1935.

———. *Joseph Conrad as I Knew Him.* New York, 1926.

———. "Recollections of Stephen Crane," *Bookman* (New York), Vol. LXIII (April, 1926).

CONRAD, JOSEPH. "His War Book," in *Last Essays.* London, n.d.

———. "Initiation," in *The Mirror of the Sea.* London, 1906.

———. *Letters to William Blackwood and David S. Meldrum,* ed. WILLIAM BLACKBURN. Durham, N.C., 1958.

———. "The Planter of Malata," in *Within the Tides.* New York, 1916.

———. "Stephen Crane," in *Last Essays.* London, n.d.

———. "Stephen Crane: A Note without Dates," *Bookman* (New York), Vol. L (February, 1920).

COURTNEY, W. L. Review of *The Nigger of the Narcissus, Daily Telegraph,* December 8, 1897.

———. Review of *The Red Badge of Courage, Daily Telegraph,* November 29, 1895.

CURLE, RICHARD. *The Personality of Joseph Conrad.* London, n.d.

CRANE, HELEN R. "My Uncle Stephen Crane," *American Mercury*, Vol. XXXI (January, 1934).

CRANE, STEPHEN. "At the Pit Door," *Philistine*, Vol. XI (September, 1900).

———. "Concerning the English 'Academy,'" *Bookman* (New York), Vol. VII (March, 1898).

———. "Harold Frederic," *Chap-Book*, Vol. VIII (March 15, 1898).

———. *Letters*, ed. ROBERT W. STALLMAN and LILLIAN GILKES. New York, 1960.

———. "Ouida's Masterpiece," *Book Buyer*, Vol. XIII (January, 1897).

———. Telegraph Blank in the Columbia University Library Stephen Crane Collection.

———. "War Memories," in *The Work of Stephen Crane*, ed. WILSON FOLLETT, Vol. IX. New York, 1926.

EDEL, LEON (ed.). *The Complete Tales of Henry James*, Vol. I. London, 1962.

———, and RAY, GORDON N. (eds.). *Henry James and H. G. Wells*. London, 1958.

———. *Henry James: The Untried Years*. Philadelphia, 1953.

——— (ed.). *The Selected Letters of Henry James*. New York, 1960.

"English Views of Stephen Crane," *Literary Digest*, Vol. XXI (July 7, 1900).

FORD, FORD MADOX. *The English Novel*. Philadelphia, 1929.

————. *Joseph Conrad.* London, 1924.

————. *The March of Literature.* New York, 1938.

————. *Memories and Impressions.* London, 1911.

————. *Mightier Than the Sword.* London, 1938.

————. *New York Essays.* New York, 1927.

————. *Parade's End.* New York, 1950.

————. *Return to Yesterday.* London, 1924.

————. "Stephen Crane," *American Mercury,* Vol. XXXVII (January, 1936).

————. "Stevie," *New York Post Literary Review,* July 12, 1924.

————. "Techniques," *Southern Review,* Vol. I (July, 1935).

————. *Thus To Revisit.* London, 1921.

FREDERIC, HAROLD. Review of *The Red Badge of Courage, New York Times,* January 26, 1896.

————. Review of *The Open Boat, New York Times,* May 1, 1898.

GALSWORTHY, JOHN. *Two Essays on Conrad.* Privately printed, 1930.

GARNETT, DAVID. *The Golden Echo.* London, 1954.

———— (ed.). *The Letters of T. E. Lawrence.* New York, 1939.

GARNETT, EDWARD. Introduction to *Letters from Joseph Conrad 1895-1924.* Indianapolis, 1928.

————. "Obituary," *Academy,* Vol. LIX (August 11, 1900).

————. "Some Remarks on English and American Fiction," *Atlantic Monthly*, Vol. CXIV (December, 1914).

————. "Stephen Crane," in *Friday Nights*. London, 1922. Reprinted and expanded from *Academy*, Vol. LV (December 17, 1898).

GILKES, LILLIAN. *Cora Crane*. Bloomington, Ind., 1960.

GOLDRING, DOUGLAS. *The Last Pre-Raphaelite*. London, 1948.

GORMAN, HERBERT. "Ford Madox Ford: The Personal Side," *Princeton University Library Chronicle*, Vol. IX (April, 1948).

GULLASON, THOMAS A. "The Jamesian Motif in Stephen Crane's Last Novels," *Personalist*, Vol. XLII (Winter, 1961).

GWYNNE, STEPHEN. "Novels of American Life," *Edinburgh Review*, Vol. CLXXXVII (April, 1898).

HARRIMAN, KARL. "A Romantic Idealist—Mr. Stephen Crane," *Literary Review*, Vol. IV (April, 1900).

HARVEY, DAVID. *Ford Madox Ford: 1873-1939*. Princeton, N. J., 1962.

HEILBRUN, CAROLYN G. *The Garnett Family*. New York, 1961.

HIND, CHARLES LEWIS. *Authors and I*. London, 1921.

HOFFMAN, DANIEL G. *The Poetry of Stephen Crane*. New York, 1957.

"Homage to Ford Madox Ford," in *New Directions 7*. Norfolk, Conn., 1942.

HUNEKER, JAMES GIBBONS. *Steeplejack*. Vol. II. New York, 1921.

HUNT, VIOLET. *The Flurried Years.* London, 1926.

JAMES, HENRY. *The American Scene.* New York, 1946.

————. "The Art of Fiction," in *The Future of the Novel,* ed. LEON EDEL. New York, 1956.

————. "Introduction to *The Princess Casamassima,*" in *The Art of the Novel,* ed. R. P. BLACKMUR. New York, 1934.

————. *Notes of a Son and Brother,* in *Autobiography,* ed. FREDERICK W. DUPEE. London, 1956.

JEAN-AUBRY, G. *Joseph Conrad, Life and Letters.* 2 vols. London, 1927.

JONES, EDITH R. "Stephen Crane at Brede," *Atlantic Monthly,* Vol. CXCIV (July, 1954).

KIPLING, RUDYARD, *Soldiers Three.* With an Introduction by HENRY JAMES. Leipzig, 1891.

MACSHANE, FRANK. "Ford Madox Ford and His Contemporaries: The Techniques of the Novel," *English Fiction in Transition,* Vol. IV (1961).

MARRIOTT-WATSON, H. B. "The Heart of a Soldier," *Pall Mall Gazette,* November 26, 1895.

MATTHIESSEN, F. O., and MURDOCK, KENNETH B. (eds.). *The Notebooks of Henry James.* New York, 1955.

MEIXNER, JOHN. *Ford Madox Ford's Novels.* Minneapolis, 1962.

NOWELL-SMITH, SIMON (ed.). *The Legend of the Master.* London, 1947.

Obituary of Crane, *Evening News,* June 5, 1900.

PAINE, RALPH. "The Life and Art of Stephen Crane," *Bookman* (New York), Vol. LVIII (December 23, 1923).

Parodies of Crane, *Indianapolis Journal,* September 9, 1896; *Town Topics* (New York), July 23, 1896.

PENNELL, JOSEPH. *The Adventures of an Illustrator.* Boston, 1925.

PUGH, EDWIN. Inscription in the Brede Place Visitors Book in the Columbia University Library Stephen Crane Collection.

———. "Stephen Crane," *Bookman* (New York), Vol. LXVII (December, 1924).

QUILLER-COUCH, ARTHUR. Review of *The Nigger of the Narcissus, Pall Mall Magazine,* Vol. XIV (January 15, 1898).

RAY, GORDON N. "H. G. Wells's Contributions to the *Saturday Review," Library,* Vol. XVI (March, 1961).

———. "H. G. Wells Tries To Be a Novelist," in *Edwardians and Late Victorians,* ed. RICHARD ELLMANN. New York, 1960.

RAYMOND, THOMAS. *Stephen Crane.* Newark, N. J., 1923.

Review comparing Stephen Crane and Joseph Conrad, *Speaker,* Vol. XVII (January 15, 1898).

Reviews comparing Stephen Crane and Henry James, *Athenaeum,* May 22, 1897, and March 16, 1901.

Reviews of *The Red Badge of Courage, Academy,* Vol. LI (January 16, 1897); *Athenaeum,* November 23, 1895; *Bookman* (London), Vol. IX (January, 1896);

Bookman (New York), Vol. II (February, 1896); *Critic*, Vol. XXIX (July 25, 1896); *Guardian*, No. 2617 (January 29, 1896); *National Observer*, XV (January 11, 1896); *Saturday Review*, Vol. LXXXVI (January 4, 1896); and *Saturday Review*, LXXXVI (January 11, 1896).

ROTHENSTEIN, WILLIAM. *Men and Memories.* Vol. III. London, 1938.

SHERIDAN, CLAIRE. *Nuda Veritas.* London, 1927.

STALLMAN, ROBERT W. (ed.) *Stephen Crane: An Omnibus.* London, 1954.

TRAILL, H. D. "The New Realism," *Fortnightly Review*, Vol. CCCLXI (January 1, 1897).

WELLS, H. G. "Another View of Maggie," *Saturday Review*, Vol. LXXII (December 19, 1896).

———. *Boon.* London, 1915.

———. *Experiment in Autobiography.* London, 1934.

———. *Mr. Britling Sees It Through.* London, 1926.

———. "The New American Novelists," *Saturday Review*, Vol. LXXXI (September 5, 1896).

———. "Review of *The Open Boat*," *Saturday Review*, Vol. LXXXV (June 11, 1898). Unsigned, but I have attributed it to Wells.

———. "Stephen Crane from an English Standpoint," *North American Review*, Vol. CLXXI (August, 1900).

WEST, HERBERT F. *A Stephen Crane Collection.* Hanover, N. H., 1948.

WEST, RAY B., JR. "Stephen Crane: Author in Transition," *American Literature*, Vol. XXXIV (May, 1962).

WHARTON, EDITH. *A Backward Glance*. New York, 1934.

WHYTE, FREDERIC. *William Heinemann*. London, 1928.

WILLIAMS, AMES W., and STARRETT, VINCENT. *Stephen Crane: A Bibliography*. Glendale, Calif., 1948.

WILLIAMS, HERBERT P. "Mr. Crane as a Literary Artist," *Illustrated American*, July 18, 1896.

WILSON, EDMUND. *Patriotic Gore*. New York, 1962.

WYNDHAM, GEORGE. "An Appreciation," introduction to Stephen Crane, *Pictures of War*. London, 1898. Reprinted from the *New Review*, January, 1896.

———. *Letters*, ed. GUY WYNDHAM. Vol. I. Edinburgh, 1915.

129

Index

Index

134